SURVIVOR!

Dan Blakemore expected to die. Every day that passed with him still living meant another twenty-four hours of stolen time. The rest of the world was content to wait for the final disaster, fighting only each other, over table scraps, but Blakemore tried to organize the Earth's resources towards a living tomorrow.

His cause seemed hopeless . . . until he met two men who were supposed to be dead! They had come back from tomorrow—come back through time—to save Blakemore for the future of the world. For he was the Survivor, the only man who could save tomorrow!

survival world

Frank Belknap Long

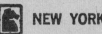

LANCER BOOKS NEW YORK

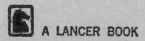 A LANCER BOOK

SURVIVAL WORLD

LANCER BOOKS, INC. • 1560 BROADWAY
NEW YORK, N.Y. 10036

CHAPTER ONE

"The call should come any minute now," Dan Blakemore told the unsmiling blonde woman at his side. "Mason warned me on the disk last night that my reprieve would be revoked before noon."

He looked away for a moment, experiencing a trace of that rending sensation which most people feel when they are required to break abruptly with a treasured moment in Time.

"But we've had our days in the sun—total freedom from strain," he added, pressing her hand. "Haven't we, darling?"

"I guess you could say that, Dan," his wife replied. "But I sometimes think we're the only two people in the world who know exactly what that kind of freedom can mean."

It had been Blakemore's first vacation in four years and he could not shake off the feeling that it might well be his last.

By digging deeply into his memory he could recall an earlier one that had been a shade more physically invigorating, but only because his extreme youth at the time had enabled him to engage, for ten or twelve hours at a stretch, in strenuous outdoor games and dangerous sports. They had embraced the scaling of precipitous cliff walls, surfboard riding and skindiving in the Bahamas, long walks over rugged terrain, and a go at archery and dart-hurling that could be hazardous if you relaxed your vigilance, and your competitor stayed alert.

At thirty-four he could still have passed for a university undergraduate and he was just as capable of resisting physical fatigue as the youngster he had once been. But when once the edge has worn off adventurous risk-taking for its own sake, inhibitions can be generated that are difficult to overcome.

All of that had to be equated, of course, with the fact that he was no longer in the Bahamas, and that most of the youths who had shared his belief that the spearing of sharks and barracudas was the most challenging of underwater sports had long ago given up and gone home.

It had to be equated, also, with what could happen if the surfboard you were riding overturned where the levels of offshore contamination had not been determined in advance. You might merely choke and gasp for awhile, with an acrid taste in your mouth. But you were far more likely to be plunged into an undertow so corrosive you'd have to shop around for a skin graft.

Otherwise nothing had changed very much across the years. The youngster he had been and his present self had both been engaged in ecological research on a Government grant and had found themselves thinking of ecology, at times, as having much in common with an abandoned puppy, barking furiously at their heels and making intolerable demands.

It was only when Blakemore, moved by a concern despite himself, picked the puppy up and walked on with it that it turned into a porcupine in his arms—a monstrous beast with lacerating quills and razor-sharp claws. It was almost as bad as having a tiger by the tail.

"When you've achieved a major breakthrough," he heard himself saying, "the feeling that total victory may be within your grasp can make putting your head on the chopping block again easier to endure."

Helen Blakemore's reply was slow in coming, giving him an opportunity to stare around him once more and luxuriate in the great beauty of his surroundings.

How supremely beautiful everything seemed, how remote from the decay and dissolution that was so prevalent elsewhere! The salt water aquarium which stood on a pedestal in the middle of the sun room was as enchanting as the view through the wide picture window before which he was reclining in a soft-cushioned lounge chair.

Beyond the pane there was a stretch of open countryside that bore a distinct resemblance to the sea, for there were many acres of golden grain ruffled by the wind, and in the far distance a lighthouse. The oceanic sweep of the vista extended for miles, beneath an almost cloudless summer sky.

But even more oceanic, in minuscule, was the aquarium, for it seemed to bring the sea right into the sun room, despite the fact that it was small enough to be encircled by Blakemore's spread arms in much the same kind of loving embrace he had bestowed on his wife a few minutes earlier.

In the circular glass bowl, amidst waving fronds and a miniature coral reef, fishes of fantastic shape and coloration, disported precisely as they would have done in the sea itself—great "Mother of Mysteries," and, of course, of mankind.

Blakemore felt a little guilty whenever he quoted Swinburne, if only in his thoughts, because he liked to think of himself as a man with no hangups dating to the Victorian Age. But great poets were, after all, ageless and it was surely his privilege to recall the immortal lines, from Spenser to Auden to Robert Graves.

Not forgetting Shelley, of course, who had had some marvelous things to say about the blue Mediterranean, the only sea that had remained two-thirds uncontaminated and that Blakemore could still visualize as it had once been while traveling in an astrojet high above it.

Why was that? He found himself wondering for the thousandth time. Had the ancient gods protected it in some inscrutable way? It seemed unlikely, for it had been on that very sea that the despairing cry, "Great Pan is dead!" had first come to the ears of the ancient world.

Helen Blakemore spoke then, seemingly in reply to what he had said a full minute previously. "There should be no need for Mason and the others to tighten the thumbscrews, as you've accused them of doing. I'm quoting your exact words. Haven't they enough discernment to realize that a man who has devoted the best years of his life to patient research carries his own built-in taskmaster around with him?"

She paused an instant, then went on angrily, "What kind of image do they have of you? And of themselves? Are they just well-meaning but badly frightened men or hooded executioners who would have been perfectly at home in the Tower of London seven or eight or ten centuries ago? I've never been very good at dates. It's hard to say, anyway, just when they first started lopping off the heads of people on a systematic scale, for failing to accomplish the impossible."

Her voice became even angrier. "Tightening the thumbscrews! Putting your head on the chopping block! If such medieval notions keep occurring to you I may have to start worrying about what could happen to the widow of a condemned man. They razed his land, didn't they? And put his wife and children on the auction block?"

If, at that particular moment, anyone else had been sitting at Blakemore's side he would have refused to tear his gaze from the picture window. But now he turned and looked directly at another vision of enchantment that most men would have surrendered the best years of their lives to without feeling that they were making the slightest sacrifice.

Surely time and change, he told himself, could never

really mar the inner splendor—yes, and the outer splendor as well—of so beautiful a woman, for it existed quite apart from aging.

"You're judging them too harshly," Blakemore said. "They're weighed down with responsibilities that they can't shoulder without help. They're simply counting on me to keep them from staggering too much when everyone is watching them. You know what it could mean otherwise. It would take very little now to start a panic."

Helen Blakemore fell silent for an instant. Then she said, "How long have we got, Dan? Fifteen years? Twenty? It all seems so hopeless."

She gestured toward the picture window, as if the wind that was blownig across the wheat field, bending the stalks erratically to right and left, had stirred in her just as great a swaying. Hope and fear, hope and fear—back and forth precariously.

"Those acres of golden grain are your personal triumph, Dan," she said. "But it was the costliest ecological project ever undertaken. It would take a century and the pooled resources of every nation on earth to duplicate it on a wide scale. Even on a limited scale, right here in the United States, it would take too long. And who is to say to one demoralized community, 'You will get enough food to insure your survival' and to another, 'You will get no food and must perish.' It would lead to chaos—and open warfare."

Before Blakemore could say anything in reply a sharp *crack* echoed from wall to wall of the sun room, and a small, black hole appeared in the center of the picture window, causing it to splinter along its entire length.

The aquarium was blown apart. As the shattered glass tinkled to the floor the water gushed forth in a descending torrent, carrying the fishes and clotted masses of bright green algae with it.

In a moment the fishes were flapping about on the floor, separated by violence from the uncontaminated microcosm that had similated a coral reef in some far-off, bright Azore.

There was another sharp crackling sound and Blakemore heard his wife cry out in frantic warning "Dan, get away from the window. Oh, my God—"

Blakemore remained for the barest instant frozen to immobility, his eyes on the shattered aquarium, as if whatever was turning the sun room into an exploding nightmare had drawn to a focus there, in the worse of all possible disasters.

Then he stiffened in sudden horror, realizing that the aquarium was of far less consequence than what was happening elsewhere. His wife was on her feet now, clutching at his arm and endeavoring to drag him to one side.

He leapt up instantly, grabbed hold of her, and dropped to his knees, pulling her down with him until they were well below the sill.

Staring up, he could see that there was nothing left of the windowpane but a few jagged splinters of glass projecting from a frame that had a smoke-blackened look. It was hard to see beyond the sill from so oblique an angle. But there seemed to be a faint flurry of movement—a kind of animated blue—at the edge of his vision. Just a wind-stirred stalk of wheat, perhaps. It was impossible to be sure.

"Stay down!" he warned, tightening his grip on his wife's shoulder. "Did you catch a glimpse of him?"

"No," she breathed. "Just a stirring in the wheat."

"How far from the window?"

"Fifty or sixty feet. Dan, be careful. He may be nearer now, waiting for you to do something reckless."

"I don't like not knowing," Blakemore whispered. "If he's up tight he won't just go away—not if he came here to kill me."

There had been a few times in Blakemore's life when so great a recklessness had come upon him that he had

10

thrust aside all caution and taken almost suicidal risks. But at such times his thinking had not been entirely without merit, for he could usually make the way he felt fit in with what he had come to believe from experience.

When the danger was immediate and very great it was often best to take unusual risks, to dare greatly and put a quick end to all uncertainty. If you wavered and hung back you were more likely to loose than to win.

Beyond the shattered pane a man bent on cold-blooded murder might be waiting with a weapon held steady—waiting for a slowly rising head to come into view. He might even be hoping that Blakemore would make himself a better target by arising to his full height.

It would have been natural enough for Blakemore to have regarded obliging him to that extent as an incredible act of folly. But he refused to let himself think of it in that way. It was undoubtedly the most dangerous thing he could have done. But it was also the best and quickest way of finding out just how great the danger was.

Unless he was met by the blast of a weapon at point-blank range or a distant shot aimed with miraculous timing and skill he could duck down below the sill again as swiftly as he had arisen and would remain in sight for no more than a second or two. And in no other way could he take in the entire wide sweep of the wheat field at a glance.

Just possibly he might get his head blown off. But that was no worse than waiting for a blast to occur inside the sun room, with a weapon moving from himself to his wife and back again, in the hands of a man who had leapt right over the sill.

Wait, and try to trip the would-be assassin up by making a mad grab for his legs as he came in? No, the odds against that would be too great. The man would be almost sure to anticipate such a tackling attempt and stay alert enough to forestall it. In a furious struggle an armed

11

man had an enormous advantage, for even if his arm was twisted and he was forced to blast at random, the shot could wreck unimaginable havoc.

Blakemore got to his feet abruptly, ignoring his wife's startled gasp. He took two quick steps backward as he arose, to keep as far from the window as possible without bringing the wheat field less completely into view. Farther back he could have seen almost all of it, but not the vital quarter-acre immediately below.

Not one or two but twenty seconds went by as Blakemore stared out, his body as rigid as a totem pole. But if the head at the top of a totem pole could be thought of as the best of all possible targets that were small in size the man whom Blakemore saw was no longer capable of realizing that.

He was at least eighty feet away and fleeing with his body grotesquely bent, his arms in flailing motion. He was clearing a path for himself as he fled, with the vegetation-crushing frenzy of a terrified animal, separated from its kill by the approach of an armed hunter.

But Blakemore wasn't armed and he had certainly not gone out into the wheat and inspired that kind of terror. It was only when the fleeing man turned once to look back and Blakemore saw how close to a skeleton he was that the fright which had overtaken him became easy to understand.

Starvation, or near-starvation, could do that to a man, strip his nerves ragged and make him recoil from his own act of violence as if it had turned into an accusing fury, relentlessly pursuing him.

Suddenly the wheat closed in around him and he vanished from sight. But the long-barreled weapon that had served him as a threshing implement, along with his flailing arms, remained visible above the wheat for several seconds longer, standing straight up like a periscope.

Blakemore bent then, and helped his wife to her feet. There was no mistaking the look of overwhelming relief

12

in her eyes when he told he what he had seen. But her voice shook and she continued to cling to him for support.

"He must have lost his nerve," she said. "Or perhaps he just wanted to frighten you, just wanted you to know that you'd be making a mistake to count on being safe here while other men are starving."

Blakemore shook his head. "He came here to kill me. I haven't the slightest doubt of it. If he'd been a better marksman his first shot might still have shattered the aquarium. But it would have passed right through me first."

"Dan, is that the image they're beginning to have of you? A lord of life and death, with a golden harvest key dangling at your waist?"

"I'm very much afraid so," Blakemore said. "And it means I've got to go after him. He's the first marauder to appear on this particular stretch of coastline. Until he's caught we won't know if the hatred here is likely to spread as fast as it did on the West Coast."

"But there's been no actual famine yet, anywhere in New England."

"That depends on what you mean by 'famine,'" Blakemore said.

Blakemore turned abruptly and strode to the opposite wall of the sun room. The thought flashed across his mind that just the fact that the communicator disk was in the precise middle of the wall, surrounded by concentric coils of wiring, made it possible for him to think of it as a target. It was an absurd thought perhaps. But centering something that you wanted to demonstrate in that way could bring it to a sharper focus in the eyes of a viewer.

"It will take him at least thirty minutes to get out of the wheat," he said. "The neutronic barriers I've set up will keep him fleeing straight ahead until he reaches the sea wall. I can pick him up in ten minutes from the astrojet. So we've time enough left to try for another glimpse of him. With eighteen visual transmission mechaniams scattered about the field it won't be difficult to activate the one nearest to him. I want you to see what he looked like when he turned—exactly how emaciated he was. Then we'll talk some more about famine—and starvation, if you wish. You may not want to."

Blakemore clicked on the disk and waited for it to light up before he began to make some quick readjustments on the remote-control dial. It would take, he knew, two full minutes for an image to come through, even if he was lucky, for the activated transmission instrument would have to pick up the fleeing man's body warmth and the precise texture of his skin, muscles and bones before it could rise into the air and follow him.

It took longer than he had anticipated, close to four minutes. But there was a compensating factor involved, for the transmission instrument had been stabilized by his care in tuning the controls until the stiplings on the V-tube had been transformed, without flickerings, into light and sound and color.

First the back of the fleeing man's head and shoulders leapt into sharp relief on the light-suffused disk, then his face as seen from in front in an enlarged close up.

Helen Blakemore cried out and swayed a little. But she waved her husband back as he started to re-cross the room to her side.

"All right," she said. "Turn if off. I've seen enough."

Blakemore hadn't. It was sometimes hard to tell, just by studying a man's face, how likely he was to be a victim of mental illness, particularly if it was the gaunt, emaciated face of a starving man. The dejected, tight-lipped, hopeless look that went with involutional melancholy was usually a dead giveaway. But a close-to-manaical look was something else again. Stark fright alone could produce it, the feeling of being trapped, with all hope of escape cut off.

14

The neutronic shields that guarded the wheat field on the north and the south could keep a man confined to a limited area, as Blakemore had pointed out, forcing him to flee in just one direction. If he veered too much a jolting shock, accompanied by a muscle-contracting spasm, could lift him up and hurl him to the ground. That the experience was a painful one went without saying.

Blakemore was sure of only one thing. No one could have been more hollow-eyed, or displayed, in the region of his cheekbones, a more parchment-thin stretching of the skin and gone on living. His eyes were not only feverishly bright. They looked like holes in a skull, filled with a phosphorescent gleaming.

Blakemore hardly dared hope that his wife would forgive him. But he continued to stare for another minute, experiencing both a feeling of profound compassion, and an anger that was detached and impersonal. He could forgive the man for trying to kill him, and bore him no ill-will as an individual. But what he had attempted to do was a threat that could not be ignored, for it struck directly at something more precious to Blakemore than his own survival and dwarfed it to insignificance.

For most of the few seconds remaining to him—he was on the verge of reaching out to click the disk off—the visual transmission instrument continued to accompany the fleeing man through the wheat, dipping and soaring like a wheeling bat with an abnormality of vision which enabled it to see in the sunlight just as clearly as it could in the dark.

Then, for the barest instant, the fleeing skeleton-figure vanished and a wide expanse of open sky swept into view. High in the sky a single, dark-plumaged bird hovered. It resembled a vulture, but could just as easily have been a crow. Blakemore preferred to think that it was either a crow or a chickenhawk.

The instant the disk went dark he made a slight readjustment in the remote-control dial, to keep it from cooling too rapidly and returned across the room to the shattered picture window.

"I'm sorry," he said.

"For not turning it right off? I didn't expect you to, really. It would have been a crazy thing to do. It's just that—"

She hesitated, her gaze accusing. "Oh, I don't know. It was all right this time. But you always seem to end by doing exactly what you want to do. It was the same way last night, when we were discussing news censorship. You knew I suspected you were keeping something from me. But you didn't want me to know about New York, Baltimore and Charleston. So you started talking, in an evasive way, about news blackouts in general—what a good thing they sometimes are."

"All right," Blakemore said. "The shipments of vegetables and dairy produce from the non-famine areas are being stretched dangerously thin, in New York especially. But there's no actual famine-stage scarcity there yet. It's only what you just said about New England that made me feel you might as well see what starvation can do to a man who's probably a native."

"So you waited until he tried to kill you before you decided I might as well know the truth. Why, Dan?"

"There's a word that may help to explain it," Blakemore said. " 'Extrapolate.' It means, of course, to take what is known and infer from it some likely future development. I've tried to spare you because it's hard for you, at times, to get a purchase on something that's actually quite simple. If the premise—the basic data—you start off with when you extrapolate is unsound, the picture you come up with is certain to be a distortion of reality."

Helen Blakemore seemed suddenly to decide not to remain angry, for her accusing look vanished.

"Dan, listen to me," she said, almost pleadingly. "I wish

16

you'd tell me in exactly what way I'm distorting reality. I shouldn't have to remind you that it's what complicates the blight that makes it so insurmountable. If it were just soil impoverishment alone—or industrial waste pollution alone—the outlook might not be much darker than it was in, say, 1980, when the danger was still being aggressively attacked on a wide scale and before human perversity brought about a kind of backlash."

"It wasn't so much a backlash as a surrender to sheer inertia," Blakemore said. "That always seems to happen when an effort is sustained too long, and the odds against it keep mounting. People—even the best minds—develop an almost compulsive need to chuck everything and go fishing. Hedonistic drives take over, on other levels as well."

"There's nothing wrong with hedonism, up to a point," Helen Blakemore said. "It can make people more tolerant, generous, willing to devote a larger share of their lives to enriching human experience and relieving human suffering."

"I'll grant you that," Blakemore said. "But the rub is— inertia is quite different from the pleasure principle. No one actually *enjoys* throwing in the sponge to that extent. Human nature isn't built that way. But when it happens there's a tendency to combine it with a wild excess of pleasure-seeking, to guard against going over the hill to the happy farm."

"But isn't that all tied in, Dan, with what I've just said? The odds have become insurmountable. Radioactive seepage from the 'peaceful' uses of thermonuclear reactors, deadly pesticides still polluting rivers and streams after half a century, antibiotic-resistant organisms increasing on a frightening scale year after year, dreadful plagues in Eastern Europe, India and China and—five billion hungry mouths to feed."

"The radioactivity isn't increasing," Blakemore said. "We can still live with it."

17

"How wonderful! So we've become sane again in that one respect. And if whales and porpoises shun the North Atlantic all the way to the Arctic Circle that should be of no concern to man. He has wings and Paris is still lovely in the Spring—if you can ignore the half-starving children."

"I could add a dozen more blight factors," Blakemore said. "But hunger is still the number one problem—the really big one. If we can achieve more of a breakthrough there—"

He looked at her steadily for a moment. "There's something I guess you might as well know. In Massachusetts people have been gathering on the Cape for close to a month now, living in shacks on the beaches, and setting on lobster traps. The rocks have been stripped bare of edible seaweeds, and the muscles lining the rocks are poisonous at this time of the year. But since they provide an illusion of food in abundance more and more people are eating them. There have been a number of deaths."

Helen Blakemore could not repress an exclamation of shock.

"I guess I don't need to tell you," Blakemore went on, "what could happen if all of that spreads to the Connecticut beaches. Every stalk of my wheat could go up in flames."

"But Dan, that's insane! Why would anyone want to set fire to it? It would make no sense."

"I'm afraid it would. Anything that's understandable makes sense, no matter how distorted the motivating factors may be. Why did that man come here to kill me? If, as you've just said, I've become a symbol of an abundance of food deliberating withheld, for selfish reasons, it would seem a cruel mockery. Smouldering resentments of that nature often lead to destructive violence, without concern for the consequences."

"But he could have been driven to desperation by just the need to stay alive."

18

Blakemore shook his head. "I don't think so. He could have made off with a few stalks without taking so great a risk. His rage must have gone deep. What I've got to find out is whether or not its just the destructive rage and hatred of a single deranged man, or a contagion that has begun to spread. There are drastic steps that may have to be taken—"

"But how would taking him captive shed more light on that?" Helen Blakemore protested. "What would you do? Give him some comparison chart tests to determine how deranged he may be?"

"It might help," Blakemore said. "It would be better than letting him escape. It would be in the hands of men far more adroit than I am at finding out exactly how contagious such emotional instability may become. Psychological probing in depth is hardly in its infancy today, despite a regression to infantalism by the background structure groups who play it by ear."

"The comparison chart technique has never impressed me very much, Dan. Grandfather felt the same way about the Freudian hypothesis before it came apart."

Blakemore had never known her to stand quite so motionless, with so tormented a look on her eyes. They were trained on the wheat field again and her voice, when she continued, had a calm incisiveness that was not in the least deceiving, since he knew how great a struggle she was putting up to remain outwardly calm.

"That wheat could help our descendants—a century from now," she said. "But—we won't have any, Dan. What's the use of pretending? It's only a matter of time before all of the lights go out."

"And I still refuse to believe that," Blakemore said. "There's something I've got to tell you, that I don't think you quite understand. It's the way I feel about that wheat and what it has cost me to grow it."

Blakemore spread his arms as if, in that sweeping ges-

19

ture, he was picturing them as long enough to embrace the entire vista beyond the window.

"You may be right in many ways," he said. "But I'll go on believing that man's best hope of survival would be diminished if anything happened to a single stalk of that wheat. In an experimental test project every stalk is important. Tests must still be made of the entire growth, and the exact extent of my success—or failure-balanced against the cost."

"But you were also thinking of something else, weren't you, Dan?—something you were afraid I might not understand."

Blakemore nodded. "It's not so easy to explain. But—well, when a man has paid a heavy price for something he can't allow himself to think that everything he has accomplished may be meaningless. Perhaps it may be. But it would be a kind of self-betrayal to let momentary feelings of despair blind him to the fact that nothing is certain, that future events may cut across and drastically change every present-day trend. No disaster is inevitable, because the historic process simply doesn't work in that way."

Although Blakemore's rather handsome features were distinctly on the rugged side, there were moments when thought gave him more the look of a sensitive and scholarly philosopher who took his marching orders from the accumulated wisdom of mankind but was not above questioning some of those orders as well, on the basis of what he had himself experienced.

"You'll never know what a price I've paid," he said. "In self-hatred alone—"

"Self-hatred? What do you mean, Dan?"

"Well—for thousands of years symbolic rites and ceremonies have been associated with the planting and harvesting of crops. The 'bringing in of the sheaves' has been a kind of glory symbol, something in which a man should take pride. It goes all the way back to the Neolithic Age.

But there have been times when I've resented every sacrifice I've had to lay on that altar. I've resented what it has cost me in peace of mind and the time I could have spent in making love to you."

"Please, Dan. Is that necessary?"

"I think it is. Or don't you agree?"

"You know I didn't mean it in that way. I meant—is it necessary for you to pretend we've ever let anything interfere with—Dan, why do you make it seem even worse than it is? I know exactly what it has cost you in other ways."

Blakemore said nothing in reply. He stepped forward instead and took her into his arms, so quickly that it would have been impossible for her to protest, even if she had wanted to. He kissed her hair and lips and eyes, lightly at first and then so vehemently, in an embrace so demanding, that they both gave up all attempt to breathe until the need to do so forced them to draw apart again.

He knew, from the way her eyes were shining, that she would have drawn him back into her arms again if he could have blotted every other thought from his mind and permitted it to happen. But he was forced to shake his head and content himself with a visual caressment of barely five seconds' duration.

"I'm drawing it too close," he said. "He'll be at the sea wall in fifteen more minutes."

"All right, Dan," she said. "But be careful."

CHAPTER TWO

It took Blakemore less than a minute and a half to descend from the sun room to the ground floor living room of what had once been a more ornately furnished summer residence, cross to the locker room adjacent to it, strip off his lounge suit and emerge into the sunlight at the rear of the dwelling clad in a garment just as flexible, but so tight-fitting that it gave him an almost frogman aspect.

He was still reproaching himself for not having kept his eyes more constantly trained on the sun room clock when he ascended into the astrojet and bent over the controls.

It had been stationed sixty feet from the house, but he had crossed the intervening distance a little faster than he could recall having done in recent weeks over a runway of comparable length. Emergencies that called for haste were certainly as much of a run-of-the-mill occurrence as the sudden darkening of the sky when storm clouds gathered overhead on a pleasant day in spring, and could hardly have averaged less than eight a month in the course of a year. But there were always a few that made you strain every muscle to outrace the clock.

In a moment the astrojet was moving straight up into the sky, where it would hover like a tiny humming bird a thousand feet in the air until he made another adjustment in the controls which would send it darting forward

—to rise higher and encircle the earth or simply to remain at the same altitude and travel toward the coastal shoreline above a field of golden grain.

From the air the field looked just as much like a wind-stirred stretch of open sea as it had from the sun room—perhaps a little more so. But there was one difference. Now the sea itself was visible in the distance, sun-gilded but not as golden as the wheat. Its blueness showed through in patches where the lighthouse towered. There was a region of whitecaps as well, and where the wind-lashed waves were cresting into foam there were glints of purple and a more tarnished kind of gold.

Blakemore was very careful, when he began slowly to encircle the wheat, to keep the astrojet from rising higher, for sharp visibility was of the utmost importance. At a thousand feet the visibility was not too good, but at a lower altitude an improvement in that respect would have been offset by a disadvantage.

It was best to get a wide view first, to take in all of the cultivated acreage with his eyes sweeping back and forth over every part of it, all the way to the sea wall. The instant he detected an unusual stirring in the wheat it would be no problem to descend instantly and hover directly over it.

There was a pair of high-powered binoculars in a case at his waist. But bright sunlight shining through a faint sea mist could be image-distorting, and he preferred to depend on his naked vision and the facile maneuverability of the astrojet. It was almost the equivalent of a body-extension, never failing to give him the feeling, when he was in the air, that he was himself in bodily flight, with a hawk-swift ability to sweep higher or lower in a matter of seconds.

The stirring, when he saw it, was close to the center of the field. It was quite unlike the stirring which was visible in other parts of the field, for the stalks were not be-ing bent in a windswept way, with just their tops in mo-

23

tion. It was as if a gigantic field mouse from the age of archaic mammals was ploughing its way through the wheat, opening up a path that did not immediately close in its wake.

Blakemore bent abruptly over the controls, and the astrojet began to descend, so swiftly that it was hovering over the stirring at an altitude of four hundred feet before he could straighten again in the pilot seat.

For an instant he was so occupied with making sure of the jet's stability at exactly that level that he almost missed his first and only glimpse of the fleeing man.

The gaunt skeleton figure remained in view for only a moment, amidst a bare patch of rust-red earth which his flight had opened up between the stalks. He was turning as he ran, his right arm upraised in a gesture of defiance, the long-barreled weapon glinting in his clasp.

It was so startling a change that Blakemore could only stare down in disbelief, without relaxing his grip on the controls, or giving a thought to the fact that to grasp them too tightly was the opposite of wise.

So the man had gotten some of his courage back!

Blakemore instantly decided not to dwell on that. It was the wrong time to let reluctant admiration take hold of him. It would have been wrong at any time, in view of what such defiance implied.

Apparently something had held the man up—probably an agonizing attempt to get past the neutronic shields—and he was still only half-way to the sea wall.

The fleeing man was clearly trapped now, as much of a prisoner as if every stalk of wheat at the edges of the field had turned into a steel bar. For ten minutes more, at least, Blakemore could safely postpone picking him up, and a thought had occurred to him that made him decide to enlarge the scope of what he'd set out to do.

If he ascended higher again and passed over the sea wall and the wide stretch of beach beyond it the time lost could be spared, and there was something he needed to

24

know. Was the beach deserted? If not, the man who had tried to kill him might have had some companions who were waiting there for him to return. And if there was a boat anchored offshore—

No, that was taking too much for granted. If the neutronic shields had delayed the man he must have tried to escape in another direction. Would he have made such an attempt if he had planned to escape by sea?

Perhaps, Blakemore told himself. It could not be ruled out. The horizontal narrowness of the field would have enabled him to get out of the wheat more quickly by heading north or south and if there had been no shields to stand in his way it would have been natural enough for him to avoid a long flight to the sea wall, circle about and return to the beach eventually by another route.

Or his companions, if they existed, might be waiting for him to rejoin them on another, more remote part of the coast. But Blakemore did not think he would have taken the risk of killing a man and depending on a distant ship to enable him to escape.

Blakemore looked down and saw to his surprise that the astrojet had already begun to ascend again, for his hands had moved automatically on the controls in response to what was perhaps the most mysterious of all human impulses—a command from the unconscious that leaps a little ahead of what is deliberately willed in a moment of heightened tension.

The astrojet had almost reached the altitude which Blakemore had been careful to maintain before he had caught sight of the stirring when a small, gray-white puff of smoke arose from the wheat eight hundred feet below.

It was dissipated by the wind so quickly that Blakemore failed to realize that the astrojet was being fired upon until a second puff arose, and the instrument section lurched and shuddered throughout its entire length.

There was a series of small explosions, all inside the jet and following one another at two-second intervals. There

25

were flames as well, and one of them swept so close to Blakemore that it scorched the left side of his face before it swept across the controls with a hissing sound and expired.

There were no more flames and when the explosions stopped it was hard for Blakemore to believe for a moment that the astrojet had been seriously damaged, for it continued on in steady flight for a full minute.

During that minute he was far from idle. No instrument within reach of his hands was allowed to remain untested. He jerked and tugged at some, reversed others, set a dozen dials to spinning, plugged in connections and listened to sounds that he recognized and a few that were new to him.

It was the new sounds that alarmed him the most. His alarm increased when one of them became very harsh and grating, like the rasp of a rusty hinge on a massive door that was being battered by a hurricane.

A great many of the instruments, including two that were vital, went dead almost simultaneously. At least, he got that impression from the way they stopped functioning the instant he re-checked them in rapid sequence.

The astrojet began swiftly to lose altitude, though it did not descend vertically but in a wide horizontal curve that carried it in the direction of the sea wall as it sank lower.

Against the altitude loss could be balanced the likelihood that it would clear the wheat field before it crashed, or was ripped apart in the air by another explosion, which would probably be quite unlike the small ones that he had survived with no more than a scorched cheek and a feeling of near-desperation.

If it came down in the sea—he could no longer hope to *bring* it down by maneuvering it—he might still be able to get out and swim ashore, since it would not sink immediately. If it came down on the beach—well, even there his chances of surviving would be greater. A wide expanse of smooth sand would provide more emergency landing space and lessen the impact of a crash.

He had no way of knowing what the outcome might be and his uncertainty had increased and was becoming unendurable when he looked down and saw that the sea wall was directly below him. He was passing over it at an altitude of less than two hundred feet.

The wall itself, with its dike-like inundation safe-guards, and the beach beyond stood out in the sunlight with a startling clarity.

The beach was the opposite of barren. It was occupied by two men and a woman, and a wedge-shaped object at least seventy feet in length that looked not unlike an enor-mous dead skate cast up by the tide, its pinkish flesh shriv-eled by the blazing sunlight and mottled gray and black.

There were clotted masses of seaweed on the beach as well and for an instant the entire scene made Blakemore think of the shattered aquarium spilling its contents in the sun room. Just why he could not have said, for unlike the fishes the human figures were not flapping about in an element unnatural to them, and he did not really think that the wedge-shaped object was a skate.

But there was still something sea-strange about what he saw, as if some unexpected catastrophe had caused the beach to rise up out of the sea with an aura of unreality hovering about it.

Then, just before the astrojet came almost level with the sand and the sunlight became so dazzling he could no longer see, the answer came to him.

The figures on the beach looked unreal because they were close to naked and the men were robustly built, the tallest darkly bearded and waving what looked like a tri-dent as he stared up at the sky. And not only was he a Neptune figure with his body gleaming with salt spray. The woman at his side bore a striking resemblance to Ve-nus rising from the waves, for her dark hair had come un-bound and was flowing down over her shoulders as the wind lashed at it. Her slender young body was also gleaming with spray from the crashing surf a few yards behind her. The other man—

The crackup was even worse than he had feared it might be. It was as if two crumbling temple walls in a grotto measureless to man had come together with a sea-echoing crash, blotting all awareness from his mind. Not all at once, but just slowly enough to make him feel that he was standing a little apart from the terrible grinding and splintering until it passed inside his head and brought about a total blackout.

CHAPTER THREE

Someone—or something—was tugging at Blakemore's arm and whispering urgently to him, repeating the same words over and over.

"You're not hurt badly—just stunned. Open your eyes, boy. Look at me. You're going to be all right."

His thinking was way out, he realized, with the buzzing that had come upon him when the darkness had lifted still making it difficult for him to do what the man wanted. It had to be a man, a "someone"—not just an object, a "something." An inanimate object did not tug at you and speak with a deep, resonant voice.

The face he saw when he opened his eyes was so close to him that he could only bring it into focus by shutting them again and reopening them more slowly, blinking as he did so.

It was not a darkly bearded Neptune face. It was a much older face, heavily lined, the eyes deep set beneath a forehead that was both broad and unusually high. The fact that it was clean-shaven brought all of the lines into sharp relief and enabled him to identify it more quickly than he would otherwise have been able to do, for he had caught only the barest glimpse of it before the crash had—

No, no, he was making a mistake. It was a familiar face, long known to him. But now it looked different somehow.

29

In the photographs the lips had been less tightly compressed, the eyes less alive, less animated by the emotional intensity which men who like to think of themselves as emotionally detached care to display on the lecture platform, or when being interviewed by the press.

Philip Faran was nodding now with both warmth and reassurance in his eyes, as if he wanted Blakemore to know that, having opened his eyes, it would be a good idea for him to just about take his time in deciding how he felt.

Blakemore felt very good. There would have been no percentage in concealing it, for there almost had to be something seriously wrong with a man who could not rejoice after cheating death by the narrowest of margins.

"You know who I am, I guess," Faran said, with a resigned shrug. "When people recognize a certified lunatic you can usually tell. Their startlement—not to say, alarm —is ten times as great as it would normally be if they just ran into an old friend tottering on a cane whom they had always thought of as only a few years beyond his first youth."

How many years? Blakemore found himself wondering. How many exactly—since Faran had dropped out of sight?

"Eight years can make a man's image dwindle more than you might expect," Faran said, as if aware of Blakemore's thoughts.

"Not if it's a certain kind of image," Blakemore heard himself replying. "You're right about one thing, though. I started thinking of you as a friend when I was knee-high to a cricket. I just barely missed meeting you in person twice, and have always envied people who were luckier in that respect."

"I'm afraid," Faran said, "that hostility, not friendship became the dominant note with most of them. But thanks for trying."

Blakemore raised himself a little more and looked

around to make sure he was not inside a crumpled mass of wreckage. He wasn't. He was lying stretched out on the sand with a firm support, probably a boulder, at his back. Standing directly behind Faran, who was kneeling at his side, was the much younger, darkly bearded man he'd mistaken for Neptune armed with a trident and a girl whom Blakemore now saw was much too young and slim-waisted to have assumed the role of even a Botticelli Venus, let alone a Rubens one. They were both wearing swim suits so body-clinging in texture that it was not surprising that they had seemed from the air to be totally naked.

The girl could not have been more than eighteen and the man looked only a little older, possibly in his early twenties. His beard was both long and forked, however, and combined with his tall stature and the trident it gave him a sea god aspect, despite the youthfulness of his features, and the fact that Neptune had taken part in the building of Troy was represented in classical mythology as seated in a chariot drawn by dolphins, and must have been almost as ancient as Jupiter his brother. Jupiter and Neptune-Jove and Poseidon to the Greeks. Greek and Roman tales of gods unaging! It seemed incredible that such thoughts could have come flooding into his mind at such a moment. The girl had sea-green eyes and there could be no question as to her great beauty. It almost had to mean that he was still so badly shaken up by the crash that a slight pinch of delirium could still distort his thinking and he did not want that to happen.

Blakemore shut his eyes, unwilling to accept what Faran had said about himself, although perhaps, in a cruel way, it cut close to the truth.

He did not think he could keep them closed for long, for Faran would certainly be tugging at his arm again in alarm before the waves that were descending on the beach could crash down more than ten or twelve times.

A famous musician had once murmured on his death-bed, "Ah, Shubert!" and expired, the tribute having come from him at an advanced age. A technological genius of Faran's stature might not stand on quite the same heights as an immortal music maker or play upon the human lyre in an ecstatic enough way to evoke an "Ah, Faran" even from the young, who might die before becoming old, but could somehow never picture themselves as dying at any age.

But to Blakemore there wasn't too much difference between the music of the spheres, and a technological inventiveness so flawless and beautiful that it surpassed what Euclid had achieved in the realm of mathematics or Kepler in his exploration of the heavens with mathematics as his guide.

For a moment Blakemore remained very still, peopling the darkness that had swept across his pupils with a host of profoundly grateful men and women intent on paying Faran the tribute that was his due.

He had earned that homage in a hundred different ways. Every one of his inventions had provided a new kind of insurance against the all-too-human tendency to write off progress as meaningless in a society that kept repeating the errors of the past and that might soon cease to exist.

Progress might not be too different from someone walking with pride down a long corridor toward a shining portal and getting his head blown off before he could emerge into the sunlight. But Faran had stubbornly refused to believe that just because ecological progress had come to a standstill for a dangerously long time some other way could not be found of staving off disaster.

It was not a belief that Blakemore could do more in that respect, since all of his energies had been devoted to starting—or helping to start—ecological progress moving again. But that did not mean that Faran was not a clear-headed, scrupulously self-disciplined thinker with every right to affirm with confidence that time travel was *theoretically* possible.

Whether such a claim was true or false, he had every right to make it. The only question was—had he gone too far in publicly stating that he was on the verge of surmounting every obstacle that could prevent a man from traveling from the present to an age remote from ours and returning again with evidence to prove that he had not been caught up in a wild fantasy caused by a head injury.

To his shame Blakemore had to concede that there had been moments when he had almost found himself sharing the conviction of small minds—that Faran was mentally unbalanced. About all he could have advanced in his own defense was that the thought had made him castigate himself severely and that the general outcry had shocked and angered him.

That was not putting it too strongly. It *had* been an outcry—an almost frenzied, know-nothing kind of protest. Faran was holding out false hopes, was adding to the general misery and despair. No man with so great a previous reputation should be allowed to put forward such a claim. It had to mean that he had become either a power-hungry schemer with an ax to grind, callous and cynical beyond belief—or hopelessly psychotic.

Faran had taken what was probably the most sensible course open to him, and not, Blakemore was convinced, through lack of courage. When a sensitive and imaginative man is accused of increasing human wretchedness and uncertainty on a wide scale he is very likely to recoil from even the remote possibility of increasing it further, despite the injustice of such an accusation.

Faran had simply dropped out of sight before the two charges—that he was insane or a cynical opportunist—could be combined and millions of unreasoning men and women had succeeded in convincing themselves that he stood condemned on both counts.

"All right, that's good," Blackmore heard Faran saying. "Just stay relaxed as long as you want to. Frankly, I was amazed that you could talk at all."

Blakemore opened his eyes, shifted about a little to ease the pressure of the rock surface at his back—he had guessed right about it; it *was* a boulder—and stared across the beach to the pounding surf. The astrojet was nowhere in sight.

"Was the jet—badly wrecked?" he asked. "I don't see it."

"What do *you* think?" Faran asked.

"It must have been. The controls were dead and it was fifty feet from the beach when the sun blinded me. But I heard the beginning of the crash."

"It went down in the water," Faran told him. "About thirty feet out. The undertow was scooping out a big hollow in the sand, so it might just as well have come down on the beach. The jet stayed in sight and we waded out and got you out before it could go up in flames."

"You mean there was an explosion?"

Faran shook his head. "No. But it happens often enough, doesn't it? In comparison with the way it looked, Humpty Dumpty would have seemed reconstructible. It's a wonder you weren't—well, fragmented. But miracles do occur sometimes. I'm absolutely convinced of it."

"Why isn't the wreckage still visible?" Blakemore asked, his eyes on the breakers.

"It broke up even more, apparently, and sank deeper—right after we carried you ashore. And the tide has been rising also, just in the past twenty minutes."

The girl moved quickly past the sea god, fell to her knees at Faran's side and spoke for the first time.

"I'm so glad," she said. "Dad's no better than Roger at concealing the way he feels, and for a moment I was afraid you might be—" She hesitated.

"You may as well say it," Blakemore told her, tempted to reached out and pat her bare shoulder reassuringly. Not because it was bare, or—at that particular moment, at least—it would have given him the male thrill that even the most fulfilled of married man is ever totally immune to, but simply to confirm, once again, that she was a woman of flesh-and-blood. The skin of a goddess would certainly have a different feel—would be marble-like perhaps, or suffused with a strange kind of fieriness.

"You thought I might be dead," he went on, knowing that if he attempted to smile he would seem to be grimacing. "I've often wondered how long it might take for someone who had become convinced of something like that to shake off the feeling that they were in the presence of a ghost."

"It was only because you looked so white," the girl said, almost apologetically.

He looked again at Faran. "I didn't know you had a daughter," he said.

"Not everyone did," Faran said. "A ten-year-old tucked away in a suburban cottage, doesn't attract much public attention, as a rule. I was always very much aware of the fact, however. They say a boy can be pretty rambunctious. But a small girl can actually be more of a problem, when you're a widower, and just a broken doll can bring on tantrums. But I guess it's been worth it."

"You know damned well it's been worth it, Dad," the girl said, but not angrily. "Why don't you tell him what a great help I've been to you."

"Right now there are things it's more important for him to know," Faran said. "A woman's indispensability can't be kept concealed for long."

He patted her shoulder as Blakemore had been tempted to do, but with a paternal simplicity that reduced to an absolute absurdity the notion that a mere mortal could be the father of a goddess.

"This is Gilda," he said, nodding. "Her name was not of my choosing. But my wife liked it, and I've grown to feel that the choice was a wise one. We could do with more Gildas today and fewer Cassandras."

Here we go again, Blakemore thought. Neptune and

Venus and now—Cassandra. Cassandra the breast-beating prophetess of despair, wailing on the Trojan beaches because the sands were running out fast and no one had known what to do about it. Blakemore had always felt that Cassandra had not been so much unheeded as used as an excuse for inertia and the wildest kind of hedonism. Yes—Gilda was certainly a much better name for a woman. What good were predictions of disaster if everyone became helpless in the face of them?

Or did Faran have something else in mind that had made him speak as he had? Was he still firmly convinced that there was no need for despair and that the twenty-first century Cassandras, whatever their actual names might be, were not helping at all?

Well, at least the Venus-rising-from-the-waves absurdity had been demolished, and the other one had begun to crumble. Just the fact that Faran's daughter had given the young man with the trident a myth-dispelling name had made the trident seem irrelevant and now Faran was completing the demolition by saying: "Despite all the pinned-downed machinery that's right at hand we didn't have a wirecutter. Without Rogers help, extricating you from the wreckage would have been more of a problem. I've got osteo-arthritis in six of my fingers. Not really bad yet, but it can be a handicap—"

"Roger Tyson," Gilda Faran said, nodding toward where her swim-suited companion was still standing motionless. It flashed across Blakemore's mind that she might have felt his full name was important, because she was expecting to share it with him. It was one of those flimsily based hunches that more often than not turned out to be wholly groundless.

Tyson seemed to possess the peculiar shyness that sometimes goes with big, husky, goal-crashing types who never seem to be completely at ease outside of athletic stadiums. He had hung back a little, as if not wanting too

36

intrude too abruptly on Blakemore's efforts at recovery. But now he strode forward with his hand extended.

"It was rugged for us before you arrived, Blakemore," he said. "Now it seems to have been your turn."

Tyson's recognition of him would have surprised Blakemore more if he had not known how extensively his image had been spread around by the media. People experienced a certain chill fascination, apparently, in watching a man clinging to a small shred of hope which they could not share and wondering how he was going to feel when it was stripped from him. Just the fact that—oh, well.

He returned the firm pressure of Tyson's hand, thanked him for what he had done and looked accusingly at Faran, who was just starting to rise.

"I've a feeling you recognized me too," he said. "Why didn't you say anything about the project—all the wheat I've grown. Frankly, nothing else is so important to me. Not even the fact that I'm still alive is one-tenth as important. Not that I'm not grateful to you, but I would have thought—"

"Oh, the wheat," Faran said. "Of course I knew who you were. But first things first, boy. Without you I don't like to think what the future might be like. That wheat was still here, in the year 2207. But if you had been killed—"

He was on his feet now, gesturing toward the sea wall. But suddenly he shook his head and his arms dropped to his side. "I didn't mean to hurl it at you like that—so abruptly, without working up to it. I'd hate to have anyone do that to me. You've got to make sure a man has some firm ground to stand on, before you shatter his universe with a single blow."

"It won't be a blow to *him*, Dad," Gilda Faran said, quickly. "He's been trying to build another universe too—by growing that wheat when everyone thought it couldn't be done."

Blakemore was too startled by what Faran had said to decide whether or not he was less—or more—startled by what his daughter had said.

The wheat—still growing in the year 2207! Gilda Faran had revealed that she possessed a mind that was keenly perceptive and unusual in so young a woman. To accomplish the seemingly impossible did mean to build a new universe, in a way—to bend nature's laws to one's will, and achieve something that was almost the equivalent of altering the basic structure of matter itself.

But what Faran had said went beyond that in a practical way, for what his daughter had said was metaphorical—a conceit of thought that took liberties with reality.

If Faran had seen the wheat a century from now it could only mean—

Could a man become so startled that it could affect his hearing? He heard nothing, but Faran and Tyson had both stiffened to an instant alertness, craning their necks as if listening to some sound inaudible to him.

It seemed to be coming from the sea wall, for they were both staring in that direction. Gilda Faran, too, was standing motionless, with her hand pressed to her throat.

Suddenly Blakemore was no longer lying stretched out on the sand, with the boulder at his back. He was getting to his feet, so swiftly that if some force apart from his volition had lifted him up it could not have been accomplished with greater posture-changing rapidity. For an instant he was convinced that something of that nature was happening to him. Then he realized that it was something quite different. It was hearing the sound at last, hearing it clearly, and that had made it impossible for him to remain for a second longer in a reclining position.

It was a shout of insensate rage, echoing back from the sea wall, soundingboard-amplified. It could only mean that the shouter had descended to the beach and was now on the seaward side of the wall.

A great wave of dizziness swept over him, fogging his vision. But through the haze that danced before his eyes he could see that the stretch of beach between the sea wall and the boulder was not just an expanse of gleaming sand with some cockleshells, clumps of seaweed and sun-bleached driftwood scattered across it. Something spider-like was swiftly crossing from the sea wall to where he was standing, zigzagging a little as it drew near.

But a spider couldn't shout and though it looked through the haze more like a spider than a man he had no doubt at all that he was about to be fired upon again by the gaunt skeleton he had pursued through the wheat from the air.

Faran's sharp cry of warning was followed almost instantly by a weapon blast that made Blakemore reel back as from a blow, and drop to the sand.

Although he had ceased to feel any pain he would have thought of himself as a dead man, with his stomach blown open, if the sand had not geysered a yard from where he had been standing. It was only that spurt that made him realize that he had not been hit, and that his recoil had been caused by the feeling that he had been struck a savage blow in the groin.

The weapon had to be close for the air misplaced by the blast to lash against him so furiously, and he braced himself for what he thought was coming—another blast so close that a second miss would be impossible.

Either that, or his skull would be crushed by a blow from a weapon that would not be fired again—a weapon a madman might well decide to use as a bludgeon, to give freer vent to his fury.

Blakemore's second fear was the one that materialized. But he saw the weapon descending and gripped both skeleton wrists before it could crash down on his head.

He twisted the man sideways and away from him, then slammed his fist against his mouth before he could wrench free. The man's mouth opened and the instant Blakeman's arm jerked back it was filled with a gleaming redness.

He hit him twice more, putting as much force as he could into the blows, and he heard the rather sickening sound of a nasal cartilage splintering.

Then hands other than his took over, and the gaunt man was no longer clasping the weapon. It dropped to the sand and was instantly snatched up by Faran, who took three quick steps backward, keeping it trained on the man's writhing torso for an instant and then shaking his head as the two struggling figures on the sand rolled over and over.

But his fear of bringing the weapon to bear again on a target that could easily have been the wrong one did not prevent him from stepping forward to intervene with the weapon reversed. He was just starting to do that when Tyson took care of it by bending over and prying the gaunt man's almost skeleton-thin fingers from Blakemore's throat, where they had gone in a last, frantic effort to reverse what the latter had accomplished by lashing out with his fists.

Lifting the still furiously struggling man up, Tyson staggered with him to the edge of the beach and sent him crashing backwards into the surf.

"That should cool him off!" he shouted. "But we can't let it go at that."

"No, that would be a mistake," Faran agreed. Although his voice did not quite rise to a shout it seemed to carry as far as that of the younger man. Perhaps there was something on that particular stretch of beach that magnified sound.

Or so Blackmore thought as he dug his fists into the sand and arose to a sitting position, hating what he had been forced to do. But it stood to reason that if he had not sent his fist crashing into his assailant's face he would not have been alive to wish that some other way could have been found.

At least the odds could hardly have been more even—a hunger-emaciated scarecrow of a man with a weapon, and an unarmed man weakened by shock and a close brush with death.

But were the odds even now? What had come over Tyson? Yes, and Faran as well. What Blakemore feared was about to happen appalled him, made him want to cry out in protest. Tyson was standing at the edge of the surf, with the trident upraised and aimed directly at the thrashing skeleton's chest.

Its three, arrow-shaped prongs made it a far more destructive weapon than a single-bladed spear would have been. Destructive in the sense that it could tear and rend, whereas a single-bladed spear could be driven home with a single, body-piercing thrust, quickly, almost mercifully. Even that would have been terrible—unless the thrashing man was some kind of monster with the lightning at his fingertips. What kind of lightning, what kind of monster could he possibly be, Blakemore found himself wondering wildly, to justify such an assault?

He was struggling to his feet again now, grabbing Faran by the arm and swinging him half-around.

"Stop him, can't you?" he pleaded, a look of horror in his eyes. "There's nothing to be gained by killing him. It's three against one now, and you have his weapon—"

"Wait!" Faran said. "You've got an almost killing grip on my arm. Could you ease it a little, just as a favor?"

Gilda Faran spoke then, for the first time. "He doesn't know, Dad—he doesn't understand. How could he?"

"He'll just have to be patient then," Faran said. We could use more of that—all four of us."

There was no real need for Blakemore to be patient, for it happened fast. But he could scarcely believe what

41

he saw. Tyson had raised the trident higher and there was a rippling interplay of sunlight and shadow on his straining back, as if the muscles were contracting as he made ready to plunge it into the thrashing skeleton's chest.

But he did not bring it downward in a vigorous, forward thrust. Instead he held it steady, and from it there came a sheet of almost blinding flame.

The man in the surf remained invisible for a moment, completely enveloped in what looked like a fireball dancing above the surf, outshining the noonday sun.

Then the fireball vanished, and he came into view again. He was rising unsteadily to his feet, his arms dangling loosely at his side. He walked slowly forward until he was standing well beyond the breakers, a vacant look on his face. So totally vacant was that look that there could be no mistaking it, even from where Blakemore and Faran were standing.

"Just his arms are paralyzed," Faran said. "The paralysis will wear off in about ten minutes, and his memory will come back. But that will give us time to make sure that he's safely behind—not lock and key, exactly, but a sliding panel that will keep him just as securely imprisoned."

He turned abruptly and gestured to Tyson.

"All right," he shouted. "Make him walk. He told us how to go about it. He's helpless now, has to obey you. But you've got to prod him a little."

"Don't worry, I'll see to it!" Tyson called back. "I can lift him up and carry him—if I have to."

"If you train that three-pronged weapon on a man's legs he can't walk," Faran said, answering the unspoken question in Blakemore's eyes. "But Roger was careful not to do that. The flare you saw is highly selective in range, and that's about all we know about it—except that it does something very strange to the mind."

Faran looked down at the weapon he was still clasping

42

and lowered it carefully to the sand. "I know even less about this one," he said. "I'm not sure I could manipulate the right trigger-mechanisms if my life depended on it. But take a good look at it. When would you say our present technology will have taken a big enough leap forward to make possible the construction of a weapon as complicated as that?"

Blakemore bent down, and made a close examination of the weapon on the sand, seeing it at close range and in detail for the first time. Not only was it complex beyond belief. There was something about it that hurt his brain when he concentrated on it, making him feel that his temples were being compressed in a vise. There were at least thirty intricately constructed parts, none of which looked exactly like a trigger-mechanism, and a few of them seemed neither triangular nor round, but in some strange way warped out of geometric alignment with— well, the way they should have looked. Or possibly it was just their metallic brightness that made them seem to blend and separate and run together again, assuming more impossible configurations the longer he stared at them.

"If you put the date about a century from now—say in 2210 or 2220—I'd have to agree with you," Faran went on slowly, "because that's when weapons like that were in common use. Also the three-pronged one which Roger couldn't have used with more precision and skill if it had come into his hands long before it did. In fact—"

Faran paused abruptly, his eyes darting to the surfline again. The man from the wheat was now walking unsteadily across the sand with the trident pressed to the small of his back. There was no unsteadiness in Tyson's determined stride.

"Funny thing about Roger," Faran said. "He has the basic maturity of a man—well, crowding forty at least. But he has a yearling colt side, and sometimes it gets out of control. A moment ago he was parading around the

43

beach with that weapon solely to enhance his image in Gilda's eyes. But I suppose few men are above indulging in that kind of harmless vanity at times. Those who can't I've never particularly liked."

He paused an instant, then added: "Roger felt that weapon went with the sea, made him feel like Poseidon. As you've probably noticed, it looks like a trident."

Blakemore had an impulse to throw back his head and laugh, feeling that unrestrained mirth was the only antidote to a coincidence so incredible that it could not be reconciled with reality. But was it, after all, so unheard of? Did it not simply confirm what he had never seriously doubted—that human thinking, on certain occasions, could follow an identical pattern in two or more individuals?

Given youthful exuberance, a robust build, and a half-humorous impulse to strike a pose might not the temptation to assume the role of a sea god prove irresistible, even in the absence of a Gilda?

There was a little of the actor in everyone, and Blakemore could picture himself in the same role, planting the shining trident in the sand with a vigorous, downward thrust and watching it quiver like a flagpole above the mirroring surface of the waves while he shouted to the dolphins to draw nearer on the rising tide.

It cost him an effort to keep looking at Faran as the latter talked, for the weapon at his feet still amazed him, and he could not quite share Faran's feeling that all would go well on the surfline, and Tyson would succeed in making the gaunt man obey his every command.

"It will be difficult for you to accept the fact that we've actually traveled in time," Faran was saying. "But a start has to be made. Since we've only got a minute or two to spare it might be better if we just thought of it as a start. I'm not sure exactly how fast Malador's memory may return and Roger may need help."

"Malador? You mean that's actually his name?"

Faran nodded. "His only name. It's surprising how many of the names we're familiar with—everyday names like Brown, Goldsmith, Henderson—have survived unchanged for well over a century. But his happens to be one of the new, unusual ones."

It occurred to Blakemore that many present-day names had remained unchanged since the Middle Ages, particularly European ones. But he experienced not the slightest desire to interrupt Faran by reminding him of that.

Faran paused anyway, shading his eyes and staring toward where Tyson and the near-skeleton figure were still moving along the beach with no change in their relative positions.

For the first time Blakemore realized that the direction in which they were heading was bringing them nearer a distant section of the beach which was familiar to him. It would have been just a sloping stretch of sand with no distinguishing characteristics if the wedge-shaped object he had seen from the air an instant before the crash had not towered in the middle of it. It was the first time he had looked in that direction, for what had happened between the sea wall and the surfline in the immediate vicinity had kept him totally occupied.

But now he saw it clearly. It no longer looked as it had in the brief glimpse he'd caught of it from the air. It was still mottled gray and black, but it had a solid, metallic look, a mechanical look that made what he had first thought it might be—a gigantic skate cast up by the tide to dry out and darken in the sunlight—seem an absurdity. The pinkish patches which were visible here and there could easily, he told himself, have been produced by—well, the kind of firing that can raise a rocket from its launching pad enveloped in a sheet of flame. It could have accounted for the mottling as well.

Seemingly Faran had followed the direction of his gaze and guessed correctly as to the trend his thoughts had

45

taken, for he was nodding now with an unmistakable look of understanding in his eyes. Although he did not even gesture toward the wedge-shaped object, his expression said as plain as words, "Yes, that's it, Blakemore. That's the time-traveling vehicle that everyone thought could never be built."

He seemed content to assume, as he went on, that Blakemore could hardly have failed to recognize it for what it was.

"We had no intention, originally, of cutting our journey short and returning without finding out what the *real* future will be like," he said. "A century is no more than an extension of the present, in a sense. There are certain to be changes. But when there's a general hopelessness—and barring some cataclysmic event that puts an end to everything—it doesn't provide enough time for the shadows to do more than lengthen and deepen."

"The real future," Blakemore heard himself saying. "Just how many years did you have in mind?"

"A thousand, at least," Faran replied. "Two thousand perhaps. Everything will be changed by then—for better or for worse. There are limitations on how far we can travel—technological ones. We cannot travel back into the past, however problem-solving that might be. I doubt if we should like what we'd find there, or that the presence of twenty-first century man would be tolerated in the past for long. It may not be tolerated in the future, but that is a risk we shall have to take."

"Why did you come back?" Blakemore asked. "Since you seem so determined to make a much longer journey I don't see why you didn't continue on. When you start to do something that takes years of planning, when it's that big and that frightening—it *is* frightening, you know —the natural human tendency is to go through with it while you're in a keyed-up, hyper-sensitive state. There are emotions that can't last and you'd need them, I should think, to travel through Time for ten or twenty centuries."

"Yes, you're right about that," Faran said. "But an unexpected technological difficulty developed when we reached the early years of the twenty-second century. Overcoming it will not be a seriously time-delaying problem. But it compelled me to balance the temptation to continue on against the wisdom of returning and making absolutely sure that nothing will go wrong. And when I made that decision I immediately made another one that seems to have been the opposite of wise. By bringing Malador back with us I felt that I could—"

Gilda Faran had remained silent for so long that Blakemore had almost forgotten she was still at their side. But now she was tugging at her father's arm and pointing along the beach, causing him to break off abruptly.

"Roger's not going to have any trouble with him," she said. "They stopped walking for an instant and I was afraid— But now he's waving. Look, Dad! He wants you to know, I think, they'll be inside in about ten more seconds."

Far down the beach Tyson was shouting as he waved, but his voice, although whipped by the wind, failed to carry distinctly to where they were standing. But there was something in his attitude that conveyed reassurance, and the few words which Blakemore caught left no doubt in his mind that Faran's daughter had not been mistaken.

In another moment both figures had disappeared from view.

"Well, that's a relief," Faran said. "When Roger's inside just five steps will take him to a compartment that has all the safeguards of a prison cell. If Malador was a criminal, which he's not, he might be able to pick a lock. But a sliding panel that can be hermetically sealed is as secure a safeguard as anything of that nature you'll find in the twenty-second century. There are a few things you can't

47

improve on much, even in an age when prisons have mushroomed out."

Faran stared across the beach to the offshore lighthouse, and a somber look came into his eyes, as if in the few places where the sea had turned a leaden gray he could see beneath the waves a lost city of dreadful night, where the buildings had turned the same leaden color and half of them were massive structures that could well have been prisons, or something worse.

"I'm sure Roger is no longer in the slightest danger," he said. "And there's something I think you should know. It concerns Malador and what I started to tell you about him. It's something I couldn't have anticipated and it's not an easy thing to talk about. But when there's something ugly weighing on your mind it's a mistake to keep it under wraps. The best time to talk about it, I think, is right now.

"If I had thought Roger couldn't handle Malador alone," he continued, after a pause, "I wouldn't have told you as much as I have. There would have been no time for that. But with a man like Roger it's not too good an idea to go rushing in with an offer of help when he's doing all right by himself and would prefer to keep it a one-man job. Unless help is needed it's the best way of convincing a man that you've supreme confidence in him, and it helps him to stay steady. Otherwise you'd just be rocking the boat."

"I could never think of you as doing that, Dad," his daughter said. "When you're in a boat—or anywhere else—you contribute nothing but steadiness."

"Well—that seems to confirm what I told Blakemore," Faran said. "Contrary to popular belief, a daughter can be more of a problem than a son. But if she can grow up believing that about you you can hardly say it hasn't been worth it. It's not true, of course. I can become unsteady right down to my soles, when decisions have to be

48

made with split-second timing."

"That's nonsense and you know it," his daughter said.

"Not entirely," Blakemore said, coming to Faran's defense. "I'm pretty sure Columbus and Drake felt that way at times." Then his expression became troubled again.

"What were you going to tell me about Malador?" he asked.

"I saw an opportunity to prove, beyond any possibility of doubt, that time travel is an accomplished fact," Faran said. "Weapons and other objects from the future can undermine skepticism to a certain extent. To a man with your background they can perhaps carry absolute conviction. I've a feeling that you are no longer wavering between belief and doubt. But in general, the belief would persist that I had the inventive capacity to fake even so complex a weapon as the one you just examined. There is no substitute for a *living witness*."

"But wouldn't the time machine itself—or whatever you've decided to call it—be just as convincing?" Blakemore asked, "If you invited someone to accompany you whose word would not be doubted?"

"I can think of no one whose word would not be doubted," Faran said. "And anyway—I would not care to undertake that kind of demonstration. I can do without a passenger who would be sure to be antagonistic from the start and might well become convinced that he'd made the trip under hypnosis or I'd put an hallucination-creating drug in his food or something of the sort."

"But could you prove that Malador is actually from the future?" Blakemore persisted. "He could be hallucinating too—or so a great many people would believe. Judging from his behavior, the safest place for him right now would be a mental institution."

"I can assure you that Malador is completely sane, unless you prefer to believe that a violent, uncontrollable rage can only occur in the insane. That's hardly tenable, you know. And I shouldn't have to remind you that we have the psychological means today of determining with absolute—or close to absolute—accuracy whether or not a man's personality is sufficiently intact to rule out psychotic behavior and the rigid, persistent system of delusions that usually accompany it."

It was true, of course, Blakemore realized, recalling what he had himself said to his wife about the comparison chart techniques before going in pursuit of the man. They could quickly remove all doubt as to whether a man who claimed to come from the future was telling the truth, since they could even expose as a fraud the infinitely complex and ingenious memory structures which believers in reincarnation sometimes came up with, in an effort to prove they could recall a thousand and one details of their previous lives.

"You may be right about Malador's importance," Blakemore conceded. "But it would take considerable time to overcome the way millions of people feel about time travel. On decision-making levels you'd encounter just as much anger and resistance. Wouldn't all that interfere with your plans?"

"It would," Faran said. "But if something should delay me, and I should need more technological assistance than seems likely at the moment, Malador—just my ability to produce him—could make me feel the way a man does when he has more insurance than he would ordinarily need. It's a good way to feel. When there's a widespread hostility you never know just how much insurance you'll need."

"Did you force him to return with you?" Blakemore asked.

Faran shook his head. "No. He desperately wanted to come and that helped me to make up my mind."

"There's something you've left out, Dad," Faran's

daughter said. "It was just as hard for you as it was for me to watch all hope die in the eyes of the hundreds of starving men and women we talked to, when we told them we could only save one of them. Two perhaps—but there would have been a great risk in adding fifty pounds more of weight—or so you told me—when the stabilizing units were giving you trouble. But if you'd been alone, with just your own safety to consider, Malador would have had a companion. That girl who kept clinging to my knees, and sobbing or the little boy with big, sad eyes who would have made Oliver Twist seem chubby. Don't deny it, Dad. You can't, because it's true."

"Starvation can be a terrible thing," Faran said. "How did you expect me to feel?"

"Thanks, Dad—for coming out of your shell," Gilda said. "I wish you'd do that more often."

"If I'd drawn further into it, or hardened the outer casing, Blakemore would have been spared what just happened," Faran said. "To come that close to getting killed can be a terrible thing too. And I don't like what I'm going to have to tell him, because it will be harder for him than it is for me to accept the fact that there's a brighter side to it."

He turned and looked directly at Blakemore. "The brighter side is tremendous, because human tyranny can't endure forever. Eventually it will collapse under its own weight and what you've accomplished will make Johnny Appleseed dwindle to a pygmy legend lost in the mists of time."

CHAPTER FOUR

Faran fell silent for an instant, and before he could continue something made it impossible for him to do anything but shade his eyes and stare past the lighthouse to where the sea had darkened to an almost purplish hue. There are compulsions which just a startling, totally unexpected sight can impose, enforcing silence with as much authority as a human voice issuing a command.

Blakemore experienced it too, the feeling that he *must* look seaward, that he could not fight against the magnet-like tug that the great ship that was coming into view around a bend in the coastline was exerting.

It was a Trawler, one of the few remaining ocean-plundering ships that every government on earth had outlawed. That its commander and crew should have taken the almost unthinkable risk of venturing into New England waters, where it could be attacked and sunk a few minutes after an alert went out, was either a tribute to a courage beyond the call of duty—if a criminal enterprise could be thought of as imposing a duty—or a testimonial to human madness.

Trawlers could navigate both rough and calm waters with twice a helioliner's speed, which just possibly might have accounted for the taking of so great a risk. But Blakemore didn't think so, for the ship would have been unable to vanish below the horizon, or slip into some nearby, cliff-walled cove in time to escape an attack from the air, unless its instruments were more sensitive than seemed likely and could pick up the vibrations from ascending astrojets a few seconds after they left the ground. Still—there were men who took long-odd risks.

Blakemore shut his eyes and for an instant was back in the Bahamas again, standing in the blazing tropical sunlight watching the Trawlers put out to sea with their flexisteel nets raised to deck-level and looking, in the glare, like gleaming shrouds completely encircling the ships.

And "Rusty" Symons was saying to him again, with an almost pleading look in his eyes: "Kid, why go back? What can that university do for you? It's just a big pile of stone that will start crumbling soon, like everything else in the north. Ecology, hell. The only hope we have left is in the sea. Why don't you join the fleet? I don't care what you say. It's the only sensible thing—the only brave thing to do."

"It's not brave to take anything more out of the sea— or sensible either," he could hear himself protesting. "The sea has to be left alone now—for three or four generations at least. It may provide some hope eventually but not enough. You won't get big catches again—of fish or crustaceans or any other kind of underwater life that's edible for a century and a half.

"The Trawlers are doing it for profit, to cash in on human misery. They don't realize it yet, but there's a drawback to that. Without ecology there will soon be no human misery left to take advantage of."

"Rusty" Symons was crowding eighty and had long ago given up all thought of joining the Trawler fleet. But most of the day and probably at night the sea remained his first and last love and he could seldom take his eyes from it.

Nothing had changed much since the far-off days of the old man's youth, for in the West Indies the flow of time moved counter-clockwise to time everywhere else.

There were still cathedral bells and masses and hooded monks and if you weren't careful a Voodoo curse could still be placed on you. Or so "Rusty" had always believed.

Blakemore opened his eyes, perhaps because a mind's gaze vision dating back seventeen years could not be recaptured for long where the northern bleakness which "Rusty" had warned him against was making Trawlers in northern waters seem remote and unreal. Or perhaps it was simply because Faran was tugging at his arm.

"They must be out of their minds," Faran muttered. "They'll be attacked any minute now. How can they hope to avoid it? If that ship is blasted out of the water I'm afraid to think of what could happen to us. We're dangerously close to it."

The ship was a beautiful sight. Blakemore hadn't seen its like for so long that for a moment he could only stare, sharing Faran's alarm in some deep crevice of his mind, but consciously hardly at all. The flexisteel nets were spread out like a fan now at the Trawler's stern, and it was moving so smoothly over the water that it seemed to be gliding past the lighthouse on a frozen plain. Even the waves that broke over its bow looked like splinters of ice glistening the sunlight, hurled high into the air by the sharp, cutting edge of the Trawler's keel.

Blakemore heard the boom of the astrojets breaking the sound barrier before he saw them. But they came swiftly into view, six almost evenly spaced dots far to the north, glittering star-bright against a low-hanging cloud.

They did not remain distant for long. There may or may not have been a rushing back and forth on the decks of the Trawler, with half or more of the ship's crew crowding the rails, for Blakemore could only make out a flurry of movement at the stern. But it seemed unlikely that the sight of six astrojets hovering directly overhead could have failed to create that kind of panic.

There wasn't much time for panic to arise, however,

for the bomb loads began dropping before the jets had encircled the ship more than once.

There was a sudden, incandescent burst of flame and a thick column of black smoke billowed skyward.

For the barest instant two-thirds of the Trawler's shattered and blazing hull came into view above the smoke, suspended in the air like a gigantic boulder hurled from the crater of an erupting volcano.

Then it fell back into the sea and the smoke became so dense that even the lighthouse was blotted out. The jets remained visible, however. They had become separated for an instant but now they were drawing together again in a tight formation high above the smoke.

The instant that formation was achieved they swept lower and headed directly for the beach, looking not unlike a wedge of flying geese.

The fact that, having already broken the sound barrier, they made no sound at all made their swift approach seem even more frightening, somehow, than it would have been otherwise, or what can strike a greater terror to the heart than death on soundless wings?

Gilda Faran pointed and then screamed, gripping her father's arm so violently that he was almost thrown off balance.

"Dad, they'll bomb us too! They must think we're—"

"I know," Faran said, in a voice so calm that Blakemore's admiration for him soared. "They think we've been stationed here with a pickup apparatus, to signal a warning to the Trawler if jets should take off. It's probably the end. We have to face it. I love you, child, more than I've ever told you."

"We've still a chance," Blakemore said, his voice considerably less calm. "Just stay where you are. *Stand very still.*"

The jets were within two hundred feet of the beach and continuing to descend. But Blakemore did not even look up at them until he reached the surfline. He dropped to his knees and waited until the distance had shortened to close to a hundred feet before he began to signal with his arms.

He used the simplest of wig-wagging codes, repeating the three-word message again and again. "I'm Dan Blakemore. I'm Dan Blakemore. I'm Dan Blakemore." Then, dropping a word, "Dan Blakemore. Dan Blakemore." Finally: "Blakemore, Blakemore, Blakemore. I'm Dan Blakemore."

For a moment he was sure that the message had been missed, for the jets continued on. They swept lower and were hovering directly overhead before an answering message came.

It came in dots and dashes, punched out upon the air.

"Sorry, Blakemore. Our mistake. We didn't like what we had to do. But trawling must be stopped. Good luck with the wheat."

The amplification was so intense that every click of the transmitting instrument made Blakemore's ears ring. He could not have wig-wagged back a reply, even if he had wanted to, for the jets had swept across the sea wall and were dwindling to dots again high in the sky before he could get to his feet. But he would not have wanted to, because what he had seen had enraged and sickened him.

Cheery good wishes were a mockery, when an act of coldly calculated ruthlessness had sent a hundred men to their graves without giving them a chance to surrender. Two hundred perhaps, for the Trawlers were heavily manned. Trawling was a criminal enterprise, but it was one thing to yield to no man in your hatred of it, and quite another to exact so terrible a penalty.

Something surfaced in Blakemore's mind that he would have preferred to keep hidden, even from himself—the knowledge that he did not like the age he was living in as much as Mason and the others could have wished. But unless a man could escape from his age entirely he had to find some way of coming to terms with it, for it was integrated with the most vital aspects of himself. Could a man perform a major surgical operation on himself, slice off much of his childhood, many of his closest friends—it was useless to pretend that some of them were not at odds with what he believed—and hope to survive. He seriously doubted it.

The pall of smoke that still obscured most of the sea between the lighthouse and the beach was beginning to thin out now. Through the dissolving haze, Blakemore could make out floating masses of wreckage. Something that looked not unlike a gigantic eel was drifting slowly toward the beach. Serpentine and seemingly in writhing motion, it caught and held the sunlight.

But Blakemore knew that it couldn't be an eel, or any other kind of marine animal.

It had to be some part of the blasted Trawler, perhaps the thermonuclear reactor that had once enabled it to take on a kind of life on the sea's surface that exceeded in its speed of motion the fastest-darting monster of the deep.

Why it had not sunk twenty fathoms deep Blakemore did not know. Possibly the blast had made it as porous as a sponge, elongating it to an unheard of length and stripping away its destructive, radioactive potential. Possibly, far beneath the waves, that destructiveness was spreading in all directions now, destroying even the few marine creatures that had escaped the Trawler's nets.

It was ironic to reject how small a thing such additional contamination had become. In the depths of the Atlantic there were—how many such sunken pockets of radio-active blight, since the first atomic submarine had vanished off Bermuda's cliffs? Twenty thousand surely, and as long as Trawlers remained on the high seas there would be many more.

For many centuries the skulls of drowned sailors had been buffeted by the tides, with a phosphorescent gleaming in what had once been their eyes. But that phosphorescence had been brought about by plankton alone. It had been a natural thing, inseparable from the sea, and not a horror engineered by man.

Blakemore did not like the direction his thoughts were taking and he stopped looking directly seaward and stared down the long beach toward the breakwater.

The beach was no longer deserted. Roger Tyson was coming toward them across the sand a few feet above the surfline, moving so swiftly he seemed almost to be running.

That did not surprise Blakemore at all. A Trawler could hardly have been blasted to fragments so close to the dark shape into which he had vanished without drawing him forth again in concern, unless imprisoning Malador had given him more trouble than Faran had been convinced it would.

Apparently Gilda had been looking in the same direction, for she was running to meet him before Blakemore could turn. Her bare feet made a swishing sound as she descended the beach, her hair whipped by the wind, and ran parallel with the breakers as she continued on, gesturing toward the lighthouse and the floating wreckage, as if she were not sure that Tyson had grasped the full extent of the disaster which had overtaken the Trawler. Blakemore doubted that he had, unless he had emerged upon the beach in time to see the jets and the Trawler before it had been blown apart.

In the moment the distance between them had shortened to a few feet and then, quite suddenly, she was in his arms. That didn't surprise Blakemore either, although up to that moment he had entertained a few doubts as to how important he had become to her and she to him.

She remained clinging to him for only an instant, her arms moving back and forth across his bare shoulders. Then they both turned and walked a little more slowly than he had moved when alone diagonally across the beach toward where Blakemore and Faran were standing.

They were both still a little out of breath, but that did not prevent Tyson from speaking the moment he reached Faran's side.

"Gilda told me that Trawler was blasted by six jets in a matter of seconds," he said. "I didn't see it, just heard the bombs going off. When I descended to the beach the sea looked the way it does now. There can't be any survivors. There never has been when there's just one ship and that many jets."

"If Dan hadn't signaled to them from the beach it would have been just as bad right here," Faran told him. "Six jets—and no survivors. We'd have been—I might as well say it—vaporized."

"But why? I can't see the reason for that. They must have known—"

"How could they have known we weren't lookouts stationed here to transmit a warning?" Faran said. "Just one look at the size of my time-traveling arrangement from the air would have convinced them that the Trawler's presence in these waters had been made a little less than suicidal by some new technological safeguard. It's a wonder they didn't blast it to fragments before they attacked the ship."

"Yes, I didn't think of that," Tyson said, his expression grim. "With me inside of it. Oh, brother! I guess I owe Blakemore just as great a debt."

He turned to Blakemore, extending a hand so huge and muscular that it would have given most wrestlers an unfair advantage. Though Blakemore had seen it close up once before and taken the risk of clasping it, he was a little reluctant to do so now, for there was in Tyson's eyes a dangerous depth of gratefulness.

There were handshakes that could be bone-crushing, and though he had enough tensile strength in his own fingers to withstand that kind of pressure under ordinary circumstances he was far from sure of it now.

Fortunately Tyson's fingers exerted no more than a firm, steady pressure, and he seemed content to let just a "Thanks, Blakemore," take care of the rest of it.

"No, Dad and I have dropped all formality," Gilda said. "He's 'Dan' now and always will be."

"I see. Well, that's fine. Thanks, Dan."

"He's quite a personage," Gilda said. "He just wig-wagged his name eight or ten times, and the jets took notice. It should still be that way with Dad."

"It was once and it will be again," Tyson assured her. "But I don't think your father attaches much importance to that, one way or the other."

"I'm afraid that's so," Faran said. "Most men have enough vanity in them to make that kind of a disclaimer sound like mock modesty. But it happens to be true. I've more than my share of vanity, I'm sure. But practically all of it runs in other directions."

"Roger," Gilda said. "We're still alive and that's the only thing that matters now. We've got to put that—that horror out of our minds."

She nodded toward the wreckage-strewn sea between the lighthouse and the beach, where the curtain of smoke had almost vanished. There were still fifteen or twenty masses of wreckage that had remained floating, most of them drifting slowly shoreward. Two of the larger fragments had been tossed up on the beach close to the break-water and another was awash in the crashing surf, where it had settled deep into the sand.

There was a sight that Blakemore had dreaded but that they had been mercifully spared—a reddening of the water where the wreckage had just begun to thin out and there was still a faint swirling which resembled a water-spout in reverse.

"There's nothing we can do now—no survivors in need of help," Gilda said. She was staring at Tyson's face and Blakemore thought he knew why there was so much concern in her voice. Tyson had tightened his lips and looked more than just troubled. It was as if he had suddenly recalled something that he would have preferred to forget.

"We'll all have to do that," Tyson said. "It's over and done with. There's nothing you can't put out of your mind if you make an effort and have no choice. It wasn't that, Gilda. I was thinking of something else."

Tyson's wind-ruffled hair—it was medium-blond with a slightly reddish cast—was cut fairly short. But it descended slantwise over his brow in a one-sided bang, and coiled around his right ear, almost hiding it. With a flick of his palm he brushed it back, exposing a darkly swelling bruise, low down on his temple.

"Malador put up a struggle," he said. "A pretty savage one. The paralysis wore off just as I was sliding the panel open. He turned on me and knocked me down. I got up before he could come at me again, grabbed him by the shoulders and hurled him into the compartment. Then I managed to get it shut before he could keep it from closing. But he tried. He thrust his arm straight out and tried to slow the panel's momentum. I'd given it a terrific slam.

"I had to grab hold of his arm and bend it back, inch by inch. If he'd kept it wedged in the opening the panel might have closed anyway. But I would have gone reeling backwards with just his arm, severed at the elbow. Both our arms could have been cut off while I was struggling with him, because, when once the panel has been set in motion, it's like trying to hold back a moving steel blade. But all it did was go about an eighth of an inch into my flesh before he gave up, whipped his arm back and the panel glided shut."

Tyson held up his arm and for the first time Blakemore saw that there was a dark stain on it an inch below his elbow on the underside, where the blood had started to congeal.

Gilda swayed a little and Faran said something under his breath that Blakemore failed to catch. It could have been a grunt of admiration and approval, or just the reverse, for it was the kind of risk that only a very reckless man would have taken.

It would have made more sense, Blakemore told himself, if Tyson had let the man come out and then grappled with him again, or gone into the compartment after him. But why even that, when he still had the weapon and could have used it a second time?

"The weapon—" Blakemore said. "Couldn't you have just stood back and trained it on him again?"

Tyson shook his head. "I didn't have it," he said. "Malador snatched it away from me when I gripped him by the shoulders and hurled him into the compartment. I think he knew he couldn't have kept a tight hold on it, because right at that moment I was getting the upper hand. He snatched it so quickly it took me by surprise. But I would have gotten it back again if he hadn't tossed it from him as far as he could, while he still had the chance."

"He could have picked it up again when you hurled him into the compartment," Blakemore said. "Why didn't he?"

"The panel was already closing," Tyson said. "Apparently he didn't have time to look around and see where the weapon had landed. The only way he could keep the panel from closing was by thrusting his arm into the opening."

"So he's locked up now in the compartment with that weapon with him," Faran grunted.

"That's right," Tyson said. "But it can't blast a hole in a solid metal wall, or even shatter the panel mechanism. Don't forget—the panel practically melts into a more massive sheet of metal, inches-thick, and with nothing he can get at attached to it.

"Are you sure?" Faran asked. "How do we know what that weapon can do?"

"He told us exactly what it *couldn't* do," Tyson said.

"He told us that a half-dozen times, but, as you'll recall, he made it emphatic when we asked him to join us in some target practice. It's not like that one—"

Tyson pointed to the far more complex-looking weapon that was still lying in the sand at Faran's feet. "We discussed both weapons when we asked him to bring down that gull, remember? That was *before* he leapt up and started for the sea wall. The rage against the wheat hadn't come upon him yet. He would have had to reason to lie to us—"

"Still, I don't like it," Faran said.

"Remember how friendly he was before he saw the wheat," Tyson persisted. "He was a gentle sort—Gilda liked and trusted him, and so did I. He was so grateful to you for keeping him from starving to death I had the feeling, at times, he was like—well, like some poor, mistreated hound dog you'd rescued from malicious children as cruel as only children know how to be—children and savages—because an unthinking cruelty is something special and apart—"

Tyson shook his head. "You know what I mean. There's a gratefulness and a loyalty that's also special and apart. I had the feeling he would have died for you—or for Gilda. That he would be capable of deceiving you about what that weapon can do— No, I refuse to believe it."

"He could have had his reasons—even if what you say about him is true in a general way," Faran pointed out.

"I trust everything he told us, *before* he became enraged."

"All right, have it your own way. But I still don't like the thought that he is confined in that compartment with a weapon we don't know too much about."

"I'm going right back," Tyson said. "But I don't think there's the remotest possibility that he could get out of the compartment. I'm more concerned about the way he feels about Dan. I never saw anyone quite so enraged, with such an intensity of hate in him. He kept cursing Dan even while I was struggling with him, and his eyes were wild."

The more than merely troubled look had come back into Tyson's eyes and Blakemore could see that Faran shared his concern.

"That's bad," Faran said. "It could lead to all kinds of complications, none of them pleasant to contemplate. We can't keep him locked up permanently and unless we can reason with him and overcome the way he feels—"

"We can try," Tyson said. "I'll talk to him through the audiotube and see what can be done. I'll remind him that he wouldn't be alive now if you hadn't brought him back with us. I think we can still reason with him."

"I'll go with you," Faran said. "He's more likely to listen to me."

He nodded at Blakemore. "Just Roger and I will go," he said. "Gilda might as well stay here with you. We won't be long."

CHAPTER FIVE

Before Blakemore could say anything in reply Faran changed his mind. He had started to move to Tyson's side, but he suddenly frowned, and came to an abrupt halt.

"It can wait five minutes or so," he said, returning to where his daughter was standing. "There's just one or two things concerning Malador and the wheat I was going to tell Dan when the Trawler came out from behind the lighthouse and we saw the jets. Until he knows how the world's tragically thinned out population is going to feel about that wheat a century from now Malador's rage will be incomprehensible to him. I think he should know, right now. That we can all come to a better understanding."

"Understanding?" Tyson asked. "I don't quite see—"

"We're going to need to draw closer together. Because when I take the longer journey I doubt that there will be just the three of us—and Malador. That will be for Dan to decide. But I don't want Dan to be kept in the dark, when it's not absolutely necessary. I can spare a few minutes more, if you'll go back and make sure that Malador isn't beating his brains out against the wall of the compartment or lying in a crumpled heap on the floor. You never know what a man so enraged may take it into his mind to do. I doubt if he's injured himself, but you'd better make sure."

"Good God," Tyson said. "What if he uses that weapon on himself? It's something I didn't think of."

"Think of it now," Faran said. "But if it will make you feel any better, I'd say it was extremely unlikely. For the first time in his life he knows what it means to be able to look up at the stars and breathe the salt sea air and stride along the beach with the sun and wind in his hair without knowing that he's going to die—and soon."

"There's more to it than that, Dad," Gilda said. "It's knowing you're with people who care."

"I think he knows we care—or did," Tyson said. "You can forget what I said about a hound dog. I didn't mean it the way it probably sounded. I was just thinking of how grateful he seemed to be—to you and your father. But if a man turns homicidal it's a little harder to care."

"That's why I don't want Dan to judge him too harshly," Faran said. "The sooner he knows the truth about him the better. All right—see what you can do. Talk to him if you want to. Tell him I'll be along shortly. If you fail, I'm almost sure he'll listen to me. If we can take just a little of the edge off his rage it will help."

Tyson put his arm around Gilda's waist, drew her close and kissed her once lightly on the cheek before he turned and headed back toward the breakwater, crossing to the surfline first, as if the crashing of the breakers had become so familiar a sound that it steadied him in some way and he was reluctant to part with it.

At any other time the tenuousness of the embrace would have amused Blakemore, for it had been quite different from the one they had exchanged a few minutes previously that Tyson must have known he could not have failed to see. But his thoughts were of too grim a nature to provide room for amusement—and anyway, it hadn't been too surprising a thing. No matter what degree of intimacy their relationship had reached, there were men who became reticent in the presence of a father and even, sometimes, in the presence of an older man. He hoped that Tyson and Gilda would not go on thinking of him in that way, but ten years did, after all, make a difference.

Blakemore was quite sure that Faran was completely happy about the earlier embrace, for he had been watching his face closely during the twenty or thirty seconds Gilda and Tyson had remained entranced, with the roar of the surf no doubt indistinguishable from the pounding of the blood in their ears.

For a moment Faran remained silent, his eyes on the tall, robustly built figure of a man who seemed to have the strange capacity—Blakemore had noticed it before—of looking just as tall a considerable distance away as he did close at hand. Then he turned and gestured toward the sea wall.

"I'd much rather start by telling you exactly what you've accomplished by growing that wheat," he said.

"Then I think it would be wise to tell you about the darker side before—well, I think I can make you see how something that seems dark for a short while can change and become a shining hope."

"What you probably mean is—you've decided I'll be needing a bandage to keep the wound tidied up. If Malador hates me the way he seems to—"

Faran smiled. "I suppose it *is* wounding—just to know you're hated by someone you've never set eyes on before, someone you've done nothing, to the best of your knowledge, to provoke. The fact that he comes from an age remote from ours doesn't make such a wound any the less painful."

"It's the feeling of unfairness it gives you," Blakemore said. "It doesn't matter what kind of man he is. When someone hates you irrationally it's hitting below the belt. You keep asking yourself why, and there's no answer."

"There is an answer, I'm afraid," Faran said. "As for

67

the wound—there won't be any flow of blood. The age from which we've just come can't deal you a direct physical blow with Malador where he is now. And I don't think you'll want to visit that age when you've heard what I'm going to tell you.

"A later age, yes—but not that one. That's why it's important for you to know what we found out about it. The early years of the twenty-second century foreshadow, as perhaps no other age could, what life on earth may be like a thousand years from now.

"If we'd traveled a century into the future and found no trace of your wheat—we'd have had good reason to feel that the battle had been lost. But we found a great deal more than a trace. Not the present field, of course, but a harvest yeild fifty thousand times as abundant.

"Not only has that field been duplicated thousands of times around the world. There are apple orchards, acres of plum, cherry and pear trees, banana and melon plantations, and fields of corn just as golden—all utilizing the soil-restoring techniques you've worked out."

Blakemore was almost sure, from the intent way that Faran was staring at him, that his expression had frozen into a strange mixture of wonderment and disbelief. He had difficulty in keeping unsteadiness out of his voice.

"I thought it might be just barely possible, a century from now," he said. "But when I considered what it would cost—"

"The cost has come close to exhausting the resources of every nation on earth," Faran said. "You see, there are still separate nations in the early years of the twenty-second century. But they are bound together in a loose confederation. A confederation of that nature gives tyranny on decision-making levels a better opportunity to flourish than would a World State, where it would have to be more rigorously curtailed. It is unfortunate that it should be so, for it is not too bad a governmental system otherwise. It has at least eliminated war."

Faran paused for an instant to stare seaward, as if the Atlantic's gray immensity symbolized for him the height and depth and width of the governmental systems which had been explored and discarded since the Dawn Age.

"There are two ways," he said, "of trying to recapture the special qualities that separate one age from another. You can set ten thousand scholars to writing books about an age in walled-off cubicles and you'll have as many volumes to consult in a surprisingly short time. But I can hardly chose that way now.

"Another way, perhaps the best way, is to try to recapture the inner essence of an age by considering how—and to what extent—its dominant characteristics may have been shaped by the age immediately preceding it. You ignore everything but the characteristics which stand out to such an extent that they fairly leap at you.

"Straight for the jugular, perhaps, like a suddenly materializing werewolf. I've said that, barring some unexpected cataclysm, a century does not provide enough time for the shadows, in an age like the present, to do more than lengthen and deepen.

"All right. Think first of the early years of the twenty-second century as an age of steadily deepening shadows. An age, also, in which technology, particularly in the categories associated with weapon-making, has taken a considerable leap forward. You can put that down, if you wish, to the desperate need that men faced with starvation have for weapons.

"Now—introduce one other factor, the most crucial one of all. The tyranny, often unconsciously motivated, and present—I'm referring, of course, to the need to exercise it—even in men of good will.

"There are many different kinds of tyranny and some of them are motivated by greed or an insensate grab for power. But fright alone can bring about a very terrible kind of tyranny. In the early years of the twenty-second century there are hundreds of men and women on decision-making levels who have become remorseless tyrants simply because of the *Big Scare*."

"The Big Scare?" Blakemore asked curiously.

"Yes, I can think of no better name for it," Faran said, nodding. "After long years of famine, of deprivation and human wretchedness, with people dying like flies everywhere, a man can become so conditioned by fear that he cannot rejoice in a sudden change for the better. Both his emotions and his thinking will have become almost pathologically distorted."

"But I can't quite see how that would make him a tyrant."

"Listen carefully and I think you will. He'll ask himself all kinds of tormenting questions. How long can an abundance of food, in a few scattered areas, last? What if some future blight should wipe out all of the gains? Would it not be a mistake to distribute even a small part of it?

"Why do some men become misers? It's usually because, in their youth, they've endured some memory-searing deprivation. To have it happen again would be unthinkable and they go right on hoarding, ten, twenty times as much wealth as they could possibly need—or a thousand times as much.

"Don't you see? Men on a decision-making level, so afflicted, can honestly come to believe that by refusing to distribute available food where it is most needed they are acting with sobriety and far-sightedness, in the public interest. All of the wheat must be hoarded and guarded, encircled by high walls that would be suicidal for a starving man to scale.

"There wasn't sufficient food being grown a century from now to justify *not* withholding perhaps a third of it, purely as a safeguard. But nothing can justify not distributing the other two-thirds to the starving. Actually, nine-tenths of it is being withheld. In some localities, the

70

entire yield. An East Indian famine at its very worst couldn't equal some of the horrors we've seen."

Faran stared out over the sea again, as if he still saw beneath the waves the city of dreadful night, but changed now from a prison-guarded metropolis to a city in which no attempt was being made to keep the inhabitants from destroying themselves as they fought with one another for scraps of food, or leapt from high terraces to the darkly-stained pavements far below.

"There's one thing I'm not absolutely sure about," Faran continued. "Did Malador recognize *your* wheat by the fields distinguishing characteristics, and realize he was in the actual presence of a hated symbol from another age that could still be attacked and destroyed? The violence of his rage is easy to understand. Up to that moment the wheat you've grown must have seemed to a man from the twenty-second century forever safe from human destruction, simply because both the wheat and the grower had ceased to exist. You cannot exact retribution from the dead. But when he realized that he had been mistaken—

"Well, that seems the most likely possibility. That he did actually recognize the field. But it's not inconceivable that he was enraged beyond endurance because, being walled in, it bears a close resemblance to the many, securely-guarded fields that had made the gaunt specter of starvation so terrible a reality to him.

"What makes me feel otherwise, however, is the fact that crude drawings of your field were everywhere. Crude—but accurate and detailed enough. They showed the lighthouse, the sea wall, the distant breakwater which looks like the skeleton of whale stranded on a sand bar, the width and curvature of the beach and even the way a few stalks of wheat tower above the sea wall on the landward side.

"Apparently the field, as it exists today, has not escaped

71

the attention of photographers with sufficient prophetic insight to know that it will soon become legendary. Microfilm reproductions of it were probably projected on wide screens, and in depth for a great many years before men on decision-making levels decided it was not too good an idea to let starving men and women dwell on something that could make them so embittered and enraged that they would demand to know why a field of wheat grown a century ago was being praised so highly when nothing that had come of it was of the slightest benefit to them."

Faran was staring at Blakemore now as if what he felt he had to say he would have much preferred to leave unspoken.

"When that kind of rage and hatred is driven underground it can take an ugly turn. *Graffiti*. You know where they are most often encountered, both in verbal and pictorial form. No one in the early years of the twenty-second century could have failed to read what was said about the wheat you've grown, for the impulse to add a comment or two to the rude drawing of some vilified symbol becomes irresistible at times.

"Hatred feeds on hatred and—well."

"So that's the dark side of the picture you promised you'd get around to eventually," Blakemore said. "You said it would seem darker to me than it does to you—and you're right. I've always thought of my wheat as something—well, rather shining. I had to. And there's nothing exactly shining about a *graffito*, no matter where it's found."

"Time's verdict will erase all that. Listen to me, boy. A man and his work may be reviled in one age, placed on a high pedestal in another. And that's sure to happen."

Faran was staring a little farther along the beach, to a point midway between the breakers and the sea wall and when he continued Blakemore was almost sure that he was visualizing as he spoke what had taken place there.

"We were all on the beach," Faran was saying. "Malador had the weapon with him. He was showing us how to operate it. We'd asked him for a demonstration, more to satisfy our curiosity than anything else. There was a gull wheeling and dipping offshore and we were curious to see how quickly he could bring it down. Then Roger would have taken a crack at it. I had no particular desire to, and, as I've said, I'm not sure I could operate it now if my life depended on it.

"He'd already told us what the trident-shaped one could do to the mind—how you had to prod a man a little to make him walk when the paralysis sets in. We never thought we'd have to use it on him. To Roger it had become for the moment just a grown man's toy—a shining gee-gaw.

"Malador had told us it could render an animal just as helpless, so that even if you were not bent on hunting down a man—" Faran shook his head, his features tightening a little. "A century from now the penalty for killing an animal is death. But the penalty for killing a man is much less severe. Sometimes no one bothered to ask what had become of a missing relative or friend."

"Please, Dad!" Gilda said. "We didn't actually see anyone being hunted down. Everything we saw was bad enough. If we keep remembering everything we heard—"

Faran nodded, "You're right, of course. It's a mistake to let it weigh too heavily on our minds. I could remember a dozen other things as bad as cannibalism, but I don't intend to. If a man is driven to such extremity that he has to cut off and eat his own—"

"No, Dad—please."

"I just wanted Blakemore to know how rare a thing it was for a man in an age like that to go to sleep at night with a reasonably clear conscience. Think it over, boy. If they committed an ugly crime against your memory and your wheat it shouldn't disturb you too much. It was inevitable, under the circumstances."

73

Faran paused again. But this time his gaze did not travel to the sea. He looked down instead at his own sun-bronzed legs—remarkable in their sturdiness for a man of sixty-three—and Blakemore was half-convinced that he was wondering how he would feel if he were compelled to part with one of them to keep himself alive.

Not that such an heroic measure would have been possible or, as far as Blakemore knew, had ever been attempted by a man in his right mind. A toe or finger, yes. He had heard of that.

"It was the first time that Malador had had an opportunity to really look around him, and take in the entire beach, the sea wall and as much of the wheat as we can see from here," Faran said. "All I can be sure of is that he stopped showing us how to operate the weapon and swept the beach with his eyes, looking toward the breakwater at first and then up at the sea wall.

"All at once he began to tremble, and gripped the weapon more tightly. He narrowed his eyes and a dark flush crept up over his cheekbones. He had the look of a man convulsed with rage. But whether he had recognized the wheat from the drawings he'd seen of it or was just enraged because it was guarded by a high wall—well, your guess is as good as mine.

"I only know that he swung around and made for the sea wall on the run, still holding fast to the weapon. He was on the other side of it before Roger was half-way across the beach.

"There were several things Roger could have done. If he had been less startled, he could have trained the trident-shaped weapon on him before he reached the wall. Failing that, he could have pursued him through the wheat. He might even have managed to race after him a little faster before he reached the wall. But you've got to remember we had no idea what had come over the man.

"Not right at the moment, I mean. Later we put two and two—or six multiplied by eighteen—together and decided we could make a pretty good guess as to what had motivated him. But by then he was far gone in the wheat.

"We figured there were several things *he* might do. He was a stranger in a strange age. Strange, that is, to him. What seemed most likely was that his brainstorm would wear off, he'd be gripped by panic, and return to the beach. What we feared most was that he might continue on through the wheat and find the grower of the wheat and—"

"He did, "Blakemore said. "If you'd gone in pursuit of him I would have been spared a lot of anguish, both mental and physical. Though I suppose you can't say that anguish can be physical."

"You mean he attacked you with that weapon once before? Good God——"

"Twice before," Blakemore said. "The first time he blasted at me through the window of the summer residence where I've been vacationing. The second time he trained it on the astrojet from the wheat when I went in pursuit of him. That's why I crashed—"

"We were just about to go after him when the astrojet came sweeping down over the sea wall," Faran said. "It took us a long time to decide what it might be best to do. We banked too much, I'm afraid, on his returning. We thought we'd better wait and see."

"That doesn't make too much sense to me," Blakemore said.

"I'd be happier if you'd refrain from accusing me until I've told you why we waited," Faran said. "Armed with that weapon and acting the way he had, I wouldn't have wanted him to return to the beach with just Gilda here to pacify him. What if he had trained the weapon on her? And that's a big field of wheat you've grown. A two-man searching party could get lost in it for hours. Of course only Roger could have gone. But he was stubborn about leaving me and Gilda here alone.

"I'm better at inventing weapons than using them in self-defense, and only he had really mastered that trident—or thought he had. And he thinks my osteo-arthritis has slowed me up a little physically, which is nonsense, perhaps. But stiill—"

"But eventually you would have gone after him? You just said—"

"All three of us," Faran said. "But the thought of Gilda stumbling through the wheat, accidentally separated from us perhaps, and with Malador on the loose— At first I refused to take that risk, and it took Gilda at least twenty minutes more to convince me I was underestimating her ability to stay alert. Then we saw your astrojet—"

A thin smile hovered for an instant on Faran's lips. "At least an hour must have passed while we were debating what to do. When you're under that kind of strain you'll do crazy things at times. The sun's still almost directly overhead, as you can see. But it was even hotter an hour and a half ago, and Gilda and Roger went for a swim, leaving me perched here like a boiled New England lobster.

"I needed cooling off more than they did, because I was angrier at Gilda than I'd ever thought I could be. She had the idea that a frail girl of eighteen could go striding through that wheat with all of Roger's capacity for endurance. Yes, and his ability to defend himself."

"Not physical strength, Dad—confidence," Gilda said. "It's a big asset in a woman."

Blakemore wasn't looking toward the sea wall when he heard a high-pitched woman's voice raised in what he thought for an instant could only be a scream.

He turned abruptly and stared, shading his eyes against the glare. Faran and his daughter swung about just as quickly.

It hadn't been a scream, but a shout. He realized that when he saw that his wife was descending the sea wall without ceasing to wave at him, and so swiftly that he

76

feared that she might at any moment lose her balance and fall.

He would have shouted to her to be careful, not to take such a risk, that there was no need for her to rejoin him in a matter of seconds when they had been separated by an astrojet crash, a painful awakening, an attack by a man from the future and his subjugation by a blinding sheet of flame—he would have shouted all that to her and more, if only inwardly, if she had not reached the beach before he could do so, and was now running toward him across the sand.

In another moment she was in his arms, straining against him, her hands entangled in his hair.

"When you didn't come back there was only one thing I could do," she breathed. "There was nothing to stop me from coming straight through the wheat on foot, and you must have known I would."

"I didn't know," he said, stroking her hair. "I've got to be honest about it. I thought you'd wait until I got back, because, after all, I haven't been gone so long."

"No? You've no idea how long it's been, apparently, or you wouldn't be talking that way. Where's the astrojet? Did you overtake him? Who are these people?"

"The astrojet broke up and has been carried away by the tide," he said. "In fragments—or so I've been told."

She pushed his head back away from her and looked steadily into his eyes, her own eyes more startled than he had ever known them to be.

"Dan, why do you always talk like that when something terrible, something you'd rather not have me know about, happens to you? If you were forced to bring the jet down and it crashed—why must you pretend it had an amusing side? You could have been carried away in fragments too!"

"All right, I might well have been. No crash could have been more shattering—to the jet at least. He tried to kill me again, from the wheat. He shattered most of my instruments and I came down in a long glide that carried me over the sea wall and into the sea, where the water was barely ankle-deep. Only some miracle kept the jet from bursting into flames. But they got me out."

"Who did, Dan?"

"I did, but not without assistance," Faran said. "It was the assistance that counted most. I'm Philip Faran. Blakemore didn't know I had a daughter, but I've always known he had a wife. The media took care of that, but I must say—"

Faran permitted a glint of amusement to show in his eyes. "It would be just a waste of time—and we haven't got too much of that—to damn the media for not doing full justice to your image on the disk. Too great a dazzlement can arouse the envy of—well, men less fortunate than Blakemore, and they may not have wanted to do that."

Helen Blakemore was staring as steadily now at Faran as she had stared at her husband. But now there was more than just startlement turning to relief and gratefulness in her eyes. Her expression puzzled Blakemore for a moment, until he remembered where he had seen that look before. He had seen it in old photographs of the men who had first set foot on the moon, after they had returned to Earth, removed their space gear and settled down to be interviewed, with their thoughts still two hundred thousand miles away, on lunar craters gilded by the sunlight and dead sea bottoms that were not really seas, but seemed just as cavern-mysterious.

It was Faran who told her everything he felt she should know, gesturing occasionally down the beach toward the breakwater as he talked. And when he had finished it didn't surprise Blakemore that it was only a moment before they were all moving along the beach in the direction of the breakwater, for Helen, as he should have known, was not going to be satisfied until she had seen the time-traveling machine for herself.

CHAPTER SIX

Time can pass very quickly just in the natural course of events, human or otherwise, as Blakemore knew very well. But it had seldom been brought quite so forcefully home to him as it had during the hour it had taken Faran to conduct them on a guided tour of the machine.

They had seemed to move from compartment to compartment—from the staggeringly incredible to the just-short-of-miraculous—in a matter of minutes, ten or fifteen at most.

Blakemore also knew that there were moments in a man's life so filled with startling revelations that the mind encapsulated them in a kind of shining cocoon, which remained apart from all other memories from the cradle to the grave.

They were standing now in a metal-walled compartment flooded with pale blue light, staring up at what Faran had called the viewing window. It was about twenty feet long and ten feet in width, and through it the breakwater and a narrow stretch of shining beach were distinctly visible.

"When once the tangential scanners have activated the warp field and the machine is in motion," Faran said, "you'll see at times just a continuous flickering. But images will appear as well. They will dissolve very quickly, however, and if you don't stay alert you could miss an entire age, perhaps three hundred years."

There were several questions that were troubling Blakemore, for he was quite sure that there must be great, enrushing waves on the River of Time that would have to be broken up or held back before you could emerge in just one particular age, one decided upon-in-advance region on the shoreline.

But before he could ask them Faran said: "I'll have to leave you for a moment. I've got to talk over with Roger the problem we'll be having with Malador and I don't think I should postpone it any longer. Considering the strain you've been under I imagine you'll welcome a few moments of uninterrupted silence."

He smiled, nodding toward the viewing window. "If you'd prefer a slight diversion instead—it needn't interfere with the silence—you might try thinking of the window as a crystal ball. Who knows? You might get a clairvoyant glimpse of the future without traveling in time at all."

Since the window had actually looked out upon the future the suggestion had a curious relevancy, even though Blakemore was sure that Faran had spoken jokingly and that his smile would have broadened if he'd thought for a moment that his words had been taken seriously.

They certainly hadn't, Blakemore told himself, as far as he was concerned. But when Faran had nodded, and left them alone, passing through a gliding panel that instantly closed behind him, Blakemore was less sure about how seriously his wife had taken the remark.

"Why don't we try it, Dan," she said. "An ordinary crystal ball wouldn't interest me at all, unless I was just killing time and there was one right at hand. But think, Dan—that window has actually traveled into the future. What if it brought back with it some undeveloped astral

80

images of the future that we could develop by concentrating on it."

"Astral! That's the first time I ever heard you use that silly word. Paranormal, you mean. 'Astral' goes with fake medium rubbish and having your fortune read in tea leaves."

"Well, paranormal then. Why not, Dan? It's not going to hurt us to try."

"Because you know how I feel about crystal-ball gazing. I thought you felt the same way."

"But you don't really have to believe it. Not in a serious way. You've always been interested in Charles Fort, and those strange books he wrote close to a century ago. About how—well, what we think are stars may be just pinpoints of light shining through holes somebody cut in the sky. You told me once that you couldn't imagine anything more nonsensical. But still, I could see that the notion fascinated you. I bet if you'd had an opportunity to test it out—"

"All right, you win," Blakemore said. "But just until Faran comes back."

Aside from the strain that it put on his eyes, staring steadily at the viewing window cost nothing, as Helen had pointed out, and for a full minute Blakemore did not lower his eyes, as he might have done if he hadn't feared that she might transfer her gaze to his face and accuse him of cheating.

Suddenly she cried out, and her fingers fastened on his wrist. They tightened, causing him pain, but the changes that were taking place where the breakwater encroached on the narrow stretch of beach were happening so swiftly that for an instant he could only stare.

The beach was both receding and dissolving, the sands running down toward the sea but melting away before they quite reached the surfline. The surfline itself was dissolving, along with the breakwater.

Everything beyond the window seemed suddenly to whip away and dissolve into emptiness, to be replaced by a flickering that was no different from the one Faran had told them about.

Or at least, it did not appear to be different, for it was occurring at intervals between a number of swiftly appearing and dissolving images.

There were barren gray wastes and tempest-tossed seas. There were crumbling buildings as well, and great stationary machines starkly silhouetted against the swollen red disk of a setting sun, or a rising one that was shedding a brighter radiance across the land.

There were black wharves and many ships and occasionally stretches of open countryside, with almost all of the vegetation looking as if it had been swept by fire or destroyed by frost or leveled by a hurricane.

And then, slowly, the land became green again, with an abundance of vegetation everywhere, including orchards of fruit-bearing trees.

When the flickering returned for perhaps the twentieth time and Helen's nails were biting so painfully into his flesh that he was forced to twist his wrist about without actually wrenching it away from her he heard Faran saying,

"The dials have been reset! We don't know how it could have happened, since Roger didn't do it. And no one else could have gotten to them, except— It certainly wasn't me and it couldn't have been Gilda."

Blakemore turned, too shaken to quite grasp what Faran had been trying to tell him.

Faran was standing just inside the panel, his pallor so extreme that if he had returned looking the same way a few minutes earlier, when nothing had taken place that could have alarmed him, Blakemore would still have had the feeling that he was in danger of collapsing.

"The machine's completely out of control," Faran went on, with an unsteadiness in the way he was holding himself that made what Blakemore feared seem even more likely. "We're already beyond the age we visited—three or four centuries beyond, at least. And there's nothing to stop the machine from careening through Time for a half million years. Do you realize what that means, Dan? *A half million years!*"

Faran might have gone on and told Blakemore more if the viewing window hadn't filled with a sight that even he could not ignore, close to collapse as he appeared to be.

It was a white and resplendent city, and it seemed almost to tower to the stars. It was the most beautiful city that Blakemore had ever seen.

In a moment it was gone.

CHAPTER SEVEN

What it really came down to was a drawing of lots to see who would be the first to go outside.

After seven hours, six minutes and an uncounted number of seconds the machine had presented them with that problem by ceasing to continue on through Time. It had emerged tangential to the warp field that Faran had tried and failed to make comprehensible to Blakemore in an age so remote in Time that there was no possibility of determining the exact length of the journey by a careful examination of the dial tapes. Faran had put it at between four hundred thousand and a half million years, but had conceded that it might be closer to seven hundred thousand years. He had insisted on allowing for a reasonable margin of error, but Blakemore had found it a little difficult to believe that a difference of three or four hundred thousand years could be thought of as reasonable.

He saw no point in arguing with Faran about that now, however, for a problem of a more immediately critical nature was confronting them.

Outside the viewing window there was a luxuriance of vegetation that wasn't just tropical. There was something monstrous about the plant life that the view revealed, something that seemed to pass beyond the limits imposed by nature on the size, coloration and structural complexity—but *particularly* the size—of flowering plants.

And someone had to be the *first* to descend into that unknown morass. It wasn't nearly as important as to who should be the second or third, for it would be the first who might be the least likely to return.

It was Tyson who had suggested drawing lots but it was Blakemore who now found himself insisting that it did not have to be with straws.

"Lot drawing depends entirely on chance," he pointed out, ignoring the skeptical look in Tyson's eyes. "And it is circumstances that determine how chance will operate. Or, if you prefer, how the dice will fall.

"Now—there are plants out there. And I'm an ecologist. That circumstance is the exact equivalent of an unlucky straw. I've drawn the unlucky straw."

It was a claim that was hotly contested by both Faran and Tyson. But the logic of it was unassailable, and in the end he got his way.

A few minutes later he was standing at the summit of the machine, on the topmost rung of the narrow metal ladder that descended forty feet to the ground.

Blakemore looked down before he started to descend and for a moment the thought that when he reached the base of the machine he might find no solid ground to stand on made him hesitate.

Was it so wild a conjecture? For several years before the first moon landing a similar fear had excercised a profound influence on the planners of the Apollo mission. It had been thought that the lunar surface might prove to be a fragile superstructure, of powdery pumice perhaps, and that if a man stepped out upon it he would break through that thin crust and plunge, perhaps several hundred feet, to his death. Just the fact that a lunar module, despite its much greater weight, had landed without breaking through would not have ruled such a possibility out, for its wide-based equalization of weight distribution would have enabled it to float as lightly on the thin outer crust as a raft on the surface of the sea.

What Blakemore saw when he stared down was quite unlike the pumice superstructure which the Apollo astronauts had failed to find and had not seriously expected to find after the lunar probes had sent back to earth data that had revealed exactly how firm and rock-stewn the moon's surface was—at least over wide areas.

What Blakemore saw when he stared down was different in a bewildering and—yes, frightening way. He had never seen vegetation quite so profuse and variegated. But though it was quite unlike the mineral superstructures the moon probes and human explorations had failed to find, it was certainly a sea—not a watery one, but a living sea of vegetation with great tidal whorls and swirling cross-currents in it—blue, green, vermillion, purple and black.

It was the black whorls that filled him with the most alarm. No, call it just acute concern verging on alarm. But under the circumstances that was bad enough. Upon such a sea a raft of light construction might have stayed afloat but hardly a man—if what he feared turned out to be true.

What if the seemingly almost unbroken surface of that sea was a delusion and a snare? Not of man's making, of course. But nature could create traps and pitfalls just as dangerously deceptive. Between the gigantic blooms of many colors—some of them were so bright he could not stare down at them without shading his eyes—and the swaying palm leaves, five or six feet across, there were—those dark areas.

They seemed filmed over with a kind of weaving opacity that changed color as it stared at it, becoming faintly bluish and then jet black again. But might it not be the opacity of total emptiness? Did not an absence of substance sometimes produce exactly that kind of illusion?

What if the first step he took amidst the blossoms and swaying fronds became his last? What if he went crashing through a flowery superstructure to land amidst a tangle of roots far below, killed instantly by the height of the fall?

Blakemore suddenly found himself thinking of it in a different way. Not as a sea of vegetation, but simply as the roof of a tropical rain forest with a towering cliff wall to the right of it where the machine had emerged from another kind of sea—the vast ocean of Time. It was poised on the brink of the precipice and the instant he descended and took a few steps forward he would go toppling over the edge and fall to the forest floor and be just as instantly killed.

But that the machine should have emerged at precisely that point, in so unusual and precarious a position, would have been too coincidental for sane belief, and his refusal to take it seriously for more than a few seconds helped him to think of the first possibility as almost equally wide of the mark.

When a traveling vehicle came to a stop after a long journey, whether in Time or in space, an emerging passenger was more likely than otherwise to find no *immediate* danger confronting him, for Earth's hazardous pitfalls were widely dispersed.

Deciding that the law of averages was in his favor, Blakemore descended all the way without letting himself think again of what might happen if he had placed too much trust in a law that many thoughtful men had questioned and with considerable justification.

The moment he reached the base of the machine and took two cautious steps forward all of his fear returned. And this time it was not just acute concern that had brought it back, but overwhelming, instantly experienced alarm.

He began to sink down. His feet sank into something soggy and the gigantic blooms closed it around him with a swishing sound, half-smothering him as they lashed against his face and threw him almost completely off balance.

87

He sank lower, throwing out both of his arms in a frantic effort to remain upright amidst the lashing. He came close to toppling forward in a head-long sprawl and might have done so if the vegetation had been less tightly wrapped around him, exerting a backward tug and his legs had not descended into the sogginess from his ankles to his knees.

The awful thought that he might have stepped into a quicksand bog made him suddenly attempt to do deliberately what he had almost done by accident, hurl himself forward and stretch out at full length on the ground to keep his weight more evenly distributed. But that had become difficult with the sogginess already tightening octopus-like about his knees and the instant he tried to bend forward at the knees and bring the rest of his body level with the ground, the backward tug of the vegetation increased twofold, forcing him to remain as vertical and rigid as a corpse being carried into ocean depths by a swiftly revolving maelstrom.

Then, so abruptly that it seemed for an instant like the total evaporation of a deadly peril in a nightmare that awakening has shattered, he was spared all need to struggle. The sogginess underfoot was replaced by a firmness and he ceased to sink down.

So firm did the ground under the sogginess become that he was able to stand on it without swaying and lift first his right foot and then the left from the sand or mud, or whatever it was the gigantic plants had needed to enable them to achieve a luxuriance that could have been matched in any age less remote in Time—not even by the great rain forests of the Amazon.

Blakemore was quite sure of that. Not in any recent age could such growths have made a mockery of man's puny attempts to enrich a soil that had not yet suffered despoilment—or after it had been despoiled and abandoned to the desperate, uncertain and even more fumbling efforts of ecologists to overcome a criminal interference with nature's capacity for renewal.

For almost a full minute Blakemore remained motionless, staring incredulously about him. Some of the blooms were intricately veined and possessed a marvelous translucency. There was one that resembled a wafer-thin circle of lighter-than-air tissue—or tissue, certainly, as light as thistledown—sliced from the center of an enormous orange. It swayed gently back and forth in the breeze, on a stalk that glowed like an amethyst, and was just as clear purple-violet in hue. Another was three-tiered, with a projecting terrace on each level that blazed with contrasting colors and if a swarm of bees had descended on it, Blakemore was sure they would have looked like tiny dancers swirling about to the tunes of a Viennese waltz.

There was a heart-shaped flower that looked not unlike the heart of a giant, torn bloodlessly from his chest and suspended high in the air on a stalk so thin that it seemed to be floating back and forth above the palms without visible support. There were two other heart-shaped blooms, not hueless like the truly enormous one, which was unique of its kind, and looking more as if they had been detached from a pack of cards used by the same giant. The smallest looked as it might well have come from the Queen of Hearts herself, for it was encircled by three golden crowns and what could have passed for a jewel-encrusted diadem.

The palms—many of them seemed also to be floating—were just as huge as the blooms and there were two that had a diameter of at least thirty feet. Some of them were as bristling and formidable-looking as the spiny cactus growths that had survived the blight in unirrigated desert areas during all the years of Blakemore's boyhood and had done pretty well after that. Others were as smooth as glass.

Slowly and carefully, while another minute passed,

Blakemore untangled the fronds that had whipped themselves about his waist, and were still threatening to throw him off-balance as the wind tore at them. It was not a strong wind for the most part. But it came in gusts, and all of the vegetation swayed when the gusts swept over it with what occasionally seemed almost hurricane force.

Surprisingly enough the feet that he had lifted from the sogginess no longer sank down into it again, and he suddenly realized that he had taken a few steps forward without being consciously aware of having done so. He was now standing on ground that still seemed a little soggy but that he could move over without becoming mired.

Cautiously, as soon as he had freed himself, he advanced a few steps more. The ground was firm enough to support him, and although he had the feeling that he was sloshing through mud or some very clinging kind of wet clay he experienced no difficulty in raising his feet and settting them down again farther on.

Apparently his first step had taken him into an unusually soggy expanse, probably one of the black whorls he had noticed before starting to descend and should have taken care to avoid by keeping its exact location in mind.

But it would not do, he told himself, to retrace his steps and shout up from the base of the machine that it was perfectly safe for the others to descend. That had to be established with absolute certainty, even though Faran and Tyson would probably start down the instant they saw he was still on his feet and was continuing on without difficulty.

For them the risk would not be too great and there was no way he could keep them from descending, unless he shouted up that he was in deadly danger and was coming right back. Since that would not have been true he saw no reason for deceiving them. In their case a warning to be careful and to test in advance every step they took would be sufficient.

But he had no intention of letting his wife descend until he had walked back and forth between the blooms for a considerable distance and in more than one direction. Not only was she more impulsive than the overwhelming majority of women, she had the foolish idea that he was over-solicitous in regard to her safety and on that account could be unduly cautious, restraining her quite unnecessarily.

There could be no question about his solicitude. But why, he found himself wondering for perhaps the thousandth time since their marriage, did some women have to be like that? What was wrong with solicitude? Why did Helen actually *resent* the fact that the man she had married loved her so much that he was tormented night and day by the thought that she might do something dangerously reckless?

He happened to know, just from discussions he'd had with three or four of his non-bachelor friends, that there were women who valued solicitude more than any other quality in a man. Why couldn't it have been that way with Helen? Weren't women supposed to want to be loved in that way? How often did it happen? Weren't they always complaining about how infrequently it happened? "Love is a woman's whole life—to a man a thing apart." But when a woman like Helen got the kind of break women were always dreaming about, she scorned it.

Someday, Blakemore told himself—if he lived to be a hundred and six—he might get to understand women. But he seriously doubted it.

He had advanced about thirty steps more and was just about to turn around and look back at the machine to see if Faran and Tyson were descending when he felt a sharp stab of excruciating pain in his right heel. It vanished so swiftly that he thought for an instant that he had stepped on a nettle or been stung by a hornet, except that it felt more like a white-hot wire grazing his foot and whipping away again.

His sandals were not only covered by crisscrossing straps in the region of his heel, with less than a quarter-inch of bare flesh exposed and vulnerable, but the mud or clay that was making his feet still feel sodden must have made that quarter-inch harder to get at. Yet, incredibly, something had pierced his flesh to the quick in precisely that spot, and now he was walking on again, too stunned for an instant to accept it as believable.

Then, abruptly, he was forced to accept it, for something cold and swift-moving slithered past his ankles with a faint, hissing sound.

Just as unbelievable as the assault on his heel was the thought that flashed through his mind as he lowered his eyes, for it was an attempt to rationalize away a probability that struck a chill to his heart, and he had never before thought that he could complete a rationalization in two or three seconds.

But complete it he did, lowering his eyes slowly to give himself just a little more time. There were hornets that built nests out of mud, and if a passing heel trampled on the entrance of such a nest—well.

It was a useless rationalization, as he should have known the instant the hissing had come to his ears. He had been bitten by a snake, and it was still in sight when his eyes came to rest on the tangle of above-ground roots, each twice as thick as its emerald-green body, between which it had started to crawl.

He bent quickly, grabbed it by the tail, and dragged it forth. In a moment he was stamping on its head, breathing harshly, bringing his bitten heel down upon it until it was flattened to a pulp.

It had been flat to begin with, because it was unquestionably the head of a snake with an adder-like aspect. A Green Mamba? No—Mambas were of the cobra family. It was certainly just as green but clearly not a mamba. A little less deadly perhaps, but most, if not quite all, snakes with triangular, flattened heads were venomous.

Familiar as he was with snakes—what ecologist wasn't —some of the rarer Old World ones he wasn't sure he could have identified from a single specimen, since the sub-species color-range varied.

Perhaps Faran or Tyson would know. Oh, God, was he starting to become irrational? If he didn't know how could he hope that they would? Still, the snake might be of some help. There were snakes that *mimicked* adders. And he might be able to determine how much poison it had carried. If it had just previously bitten some small animal its poison sacs might have been depleted. Smashing its head had been a stupid thing to do. It would make that harder to determine.

He should have gripped the back of its head just below its mouth as he'd once seen a herpetologist do with a Fer-de-lance, and carried it intact, and despite its thrashings, back to the machine.

But he picked it up anyway, and flung it over his arm, still quivering and with its head so crushed that it no longer looked triangular.

He had almost covered the distance he had traveled over ground that had turned out to be as dangerous as he had feared it might be, but in a different way, when he saw Faran waving and staring down at him from near the summit of the machine. He had just started to descend and there was a puzzled, slightly angry look on his face, distinguishable even from a distance of forty feet.

"What kept you so long?" he called down. "We couldn't see you at all for a minute or two. This is the wrong time for ecological research."

"I've been bitten by a snake," Blakemore shouted back. "A venomous one, I think. I'm carrying it. Didn't you notice?"

93

"Yes, I see it now. For God's sake, boy, get up here as quickly as you can. We've got to do some fast cutting."

It took Blakemore close to half a minute to ascend to where Faran was standing, for he had to transfer the snake from his right to his left arm, and once it almost caught on one of the ladder rungs.

He was a little out of breath when he reached Faran's side and the older man was breathing harshly too, but not from exertion, and his face was drained of all color.

"Get inside," he urged. "Hurry. We've got to make some deep incisions and apply a tourniquet. Poisonous snakes are far rarer than harmless ones. What makes you think it's venomous?"

It was true, of course—wildly, fantastically so. They were far rarer, which meant that anyone who trusted the law of averages was backing a horse of the wrong color. To encounter a venomous snake a few minutes after you emerged in a world remote from ours was as unlikely as that the machine could have come out on the brink of a precipice. Of the two possibilities it was probably the unlikeliest. But that meant nothing at all, since it was the one that had happened.

"It had the flat, triangular head of an Old World viper," Blakemore heard himself saying. "It's crushed now, so you can't see it."

"All right, don't talk. Just get inside. The quicker we get the tourniquet on the better.

It was good advice, but Blakemore found himself under a compulsion to add: "My chances may not be too good. The venom could be cobra-deadly."

"An adder's isn't. Neither is a copperhead's or a rattlesnake's. Even a cobra— Listen, boy. *You* ought to know that. All the accounts are exaggerated—from the Black Widow spider on up. A centipede's bite, for instance, is hardly worse than a bee sting, as a rule. Do you feel all right, so far?"

Blakemore managed to nod.

"Good. A cobra's venom is a nerve poison, quick acting. Get rid of that fear right now and get inside."

Blakemore nodded and ascended the seven remaining rungs of the ladder, with Faran holding on to the arm over which the snake was draped to steady him.

CHAPTER EIGHT

The worst thing of all was the crowding. Being human, there was nothing that Blakemore ordinarily appreciated more than sympathy. And the look in his wife's eyes completely transcended the kind of very real concern displayed by Gilda and Tyson. It was the kind of solicitude that could only mean that if he died she would die too, at least inwardly and would never be the same again this side of eternity. It was exactly the kind of solicitude that she resented when it was directed in the opposite direction. But now he could even forgive that strange quirk in her nature.

If it hadn't been for the crowding—

They were all clustering so closely about him that Faran was having difficulty in making the incisions, for he had to keep stopping to gesture them back. And it gave him a smothering feeling even though neither Gilda nor his wife was standing that close to him, and Tyson was at least three feet away.

He lay stretched out at full length on a metal cot and Faran was setting to work on his heel first, seeming to feel that the first order of business was to get the venom still lingering at the site of the wound out, as quickly as possible. He had made two crosswise cuts and was just bending to apply his lips to the wound when Helen brushed past him and knelt beside the cot.

"Here, let me do that," she said.

Blakemore looked at Faran, raising himself a little, his hand going to his wife's shoulder to push her gently back.

"Is—is it dangerous?" he asked.

Faran shook his head, smiling wryly. "If it was me—you'd have let me take the risk," he said. "I'm surprised an ecologist wouldn't know the risks are negligible. You must have seen it done before."

"Once or twice," Blakemore said. "I knew, in a way, but—sometimes you don't think."

"It's all right," Faran said. "Naturally you're more concerned about Helen than anyone else. But if you'd thought it was dangerous I don't think you'd have been too happy about letting me kill myself."

"Christ, no," Blakemore said.

"So—all's forgiven."

He tapped Helen gently on the shoulder. "There may not be any venom," he said. "But we don't know, so we can't take a chance. The greatest concentration is still at the site of the puncture. Only ten or twelve minutes have elapsed, so not much of the venom may have—well, we can only wait and see. Just keep drawing the blood into your mouth and spitting it out. I'll tell you when to stop."

When Helen had finished she stood up, pressed her husband's arm and stood back, her shoulders shaking a little.

The tourniquet was just a splinter of wood and a cloth bandage bound so tightly around Blakemore's leg to stop the flow of arterial blood that he winced when Faran was applying it. Despite the way he felt it amused him a little to realize that the wooden splinter—it was peg-shaped, with a lizard-like head—came from the sea. It was one of the small, grotesquely shaped fragments of driftwood that Roger had picked up, along with the few rare and exquisitely beautiful shells that were sometimes cast up on non-tropical beaches, and which he had seemingly been unable to resist.

"The earliest ones were made of rubber," Faran said. "Esmarch's is perhaps the best, in principle, but just a torn-up sheet has saved as many lives. More perhaps, because when people come staggering in after a snake bite, ripping a sheet off a bed is the first thing that comes to mind. Anything that puts a big dent in the circulation will do as well."

He paused an instant, then asked: "How do you feel now, boy? Be honest about it."

"I'm not sure," Blakemore said. "All right, I guess. There's a slight dizziness, but that could just come from the strain."

"And the excitement," he added, with a thin smile.

"We may well be getting excited about nothing," Faran said. "That snake could be as harmless as—well, a garter snake or a black snake. Look—I read somewhere that there are two harmless snakes that look exactly like adders. Protective mimicry. 'Don't tread on me because you know what an adder can do to you. You've got to believe me. Look at my flat head.' "

"I thought of that," Blakemore said. "I guess there's nothing I didn't think of."

"That kind of protective mimicry could save the lives of a lot of people I've met too, Dad," Gilda said.

"I don't think it's too good an idea to flaunt the colors of malignancy," Faran said. "In the end—you get your head flattened out even more."

"It's damned unfortunate we haven't some snake-bite serum," Tyson said. "But since you can't positively identify the snake it might have been the wrong kind anyway."

"Quite possibly it would have been," Faran agreed. "But since it would have done no harm, I would have injected it immediately. That's like saying it would be nice if you could carry a collapsible medical clinic around with you which you could blow up like a toy balloon in the event of an emergency.

As if feeling that what he had said was not as reassuring as it should have been he pressed Blakemore's shoulder and went on thoughtfully: "I'm not at all seriously worried. Let's put it this way. Unless the snake is a cobra, quickly applied emergency measures are extraordinarily effective. You may have a few bad moments—be as ill as you would be if you came down with a light to middling attack of influenza. It may last for a few days. I just don't know. But the fact that you still don't feel ill at all —you can write off the slight dizziness—is highly encouraging."

"If a coral snake had bitten me I'd be dead by now, is that what you mean?"

Faran shook his head. "No, contrary to popular belief, there may have been many coral snake recoveries, despite the fact that it is almost as poisonous as a King Cobra. But a coral snake didn't bite you—"

He sighed. "I keep forgetting you know much more about snakes than I do. But that's good, in a way—it means you know that everything I've told you is the truth. You either won't become ill at all, because the snake was harmless or—"

Helen Blakemore cut him short, her voice rising a little.

"There's something I'm waiting to hear both of you say. That there's not the remotest chance that you're both mistaken. That it's not going to be *very bad*."

She covered her face with her hands, and Blakemore was sure that she had not wanted to come out with that, that she would rather have bitten her tongue off.

"There's always that possibility, darling," Blakemore said. "Philip knows that—and so do you. But there's something else you're forgetting. The thread can be cut at any time, for anyone, young or old, and it happens so often that it's just as well we can't see how close to the precipice edge we're standing every day of our lives. Let's say I've just moved a few steps nearer, on this one

99

particular day. But everyone does that constantly without even being aware of it."

Faran made no attempt to dispute what Blakemore had said. Instead he turned abruptly, and spoke directly to Gilda and Tyson. "Dan needs rest now—as much of it as he can get between now and tomorrow. So please vanish, both of you. Helen can stay with him as long as she wants to, but I'm hoping she won't want to. There are times when it's best for a man to be absolutely alone."

"I'm not sure about that," Helen Blakemore said. "But I think I know what you mean. I'll go too. So will you, I suppose."

Faran nodded. "Of course."

He looked at Blakemore.

"The communicator is right there—at your elbow. I'm suggesting this for your own good. You must avoid the slightest exertion or emotional strain for awhile. Lie back and close your eyes. Try to get some sleep. We want to keep your circulation as stabilized as possible."

"All right, I'll try," Blakemore said.

It hit him an hour and a half later. Stomach cramps at first and then darting pains in his arms and legs. He reached for the communicator but almost immediately changed his mind, bringing his hand back to his side.

Better to wait and find out how bad it was going to be. It was still not very bad and perhaps if he waited the pains would go away. He must not alarm Helen unless it became absolutely necessary.

Besides, what could Faran possibly do? There was no remedy that could change the course of snake-bite illness after emergency measures had been applied, except a serum that he was separated from by a wide waste of years.

Whiskey? That wasn't a remedy at all, but a lethal way of making sure that a bitten man's chances of survival would be cut in half. It sent the poisoned blood coursing

100

through every artery and vein and the harm it could do had been known for close to a century. It was as bad, if not worse, than the once widely practiced medical insanity of putting a man with cirrhosis of the liver on a starvation diet.

He would simply have to endure it as long as he could, and after that, if the pains did not ease, accept the fact that a viper's bite could kill, as it so often had.

The bite of any poisonous snake could kill, and in the absence of emergency measures was more likely to do so than otherwise, despite what Faran had tried to make him believe. And even with emergency measures—the fatalities were legion.

True, such bites could be almost as inconsequential as bee stings at times, but even bee stings could kill. It depended on the individual, his constitutional peculiarities, the freakishness with which any poisonous substance introduced into the body could bring about changes in the victim's vital organs before making its exit.

The pains in Blakemore's limbs began to get worse, to march along in company with the dark turn his thoughts were taking.

If nothing that Faran could do was going to help him, using the communicator would make very little sense. To have his wife at his side was the only good that could come of it. But it would be a wholly selfish kind of benefit and would bring her nothing but pain. To be forced to watch him suffer and be powerless to ease his torment —Had he any right to make her undergo such an ordeal?

Was he going to die? If he was he would, of course, want her to be with him when the end came. But until that moment came, until his desire to spare her cracked under his terrible, human need—as of course it would— it was surely better to fight on alone.

It wouldn't be easy, but he felt that he could do it if he turned his face to the wall, drew up his knees and forced himself not to think of just how bad the pain had become, and how likely it was that a pain that started in a leg or an arm would not stay confined to a limb. It would almost certainly spread to his chest and interfere with his breathing and he would soon begin to feel a constriction about his heart.

It didn't seem to be happening, however. There were just the darting pains, and he could still draw a deep breath and hold it, and there was even a slight improvement in the way he felt, for the stomach cramps had gone away.

He had not even considered the possibility that what he might have most to fear was the spread of the toxins in his bloodstream to the cells of his brain. He had no premonition concerning that at all, no forewarning, and when it happened he had no way of knowing that it had taken place, because he passed so swiftly from an awareness of his immediate surroundings into a gray world of vast, stationary shadows that it seemed perfectly natural to him to be standing in the midst of towering gray monoliths covered with indecipherable inscriptions carven into the stone.

It was not strictly true, perhaps, to say that he had no awareness of the fact that everything about him had undergone a change. It was only that it all seemed so natural to him that it was hard for him to think of it as a change.

There was a mountain too—a high, domed mountain with something shadowy and enormous bisecting it from its base to its summit, but he could not quite make out what the something was.

A voice seemed to whisper to him that it might be just as well for him not to know, that it was a secret as old as Time itself.

Long ages seemed to sweep by as he stood staring up at the towering monoliths and the mountain in the near distance. There was no sign of human life anywhere or any stir of movement that might have revealed the presence of some great beast lurking in shadows that could tear and rend.

Yet—and this disturbed without frightening him as it should have done—he had the feeling that he was being watched by invisible eyes which might well have been the eyes of some great, hidden beast.

Why was his fear not more acute? Was it because everything in proximity to him did not seem quite real enough to be firmly grasped, either by his hands if he should reach out and attempt to find out whether he was dreaming or awake, or by his mind if he brought his vision to a sharper focus and the shadows changed into something else?

Somehow he was incapable of doing that, of testing the reality of everything he saw in that way.

Then, quite suddenly, all of the shadows began to deepen and a curtain of blackness swept down over the monoliths. It was almost as if he were watching a play on a lighted stage, and the end of the final act had come. But that would not have been strictly true, because there had been no light behind the curtain bright enough to be cast by footlights even if the rest of the stage had been dark.

It had never been more than a kind of half-light that had seemed on the verge of vanishing even when he had been able to make out by straining his eyes, the outlines of the domed mountain and the shadowy shape bisecting it from its base to its summit.

And yet—it was a paradox that verged on the insane —he had actually been able to make out the inscriptions engraved on the monoliths, so distinctly that the configuration of every character had stood out with a startling clarity. He had been able to determine how impossible it would have been for him to decipher them, for although they bore a slight resemblance to Egyptian hieroglyphics the resemblance was tenuous at best and probably non-existent. Deciphering Egyptian hieroglyphics would have been beyond him anyway, except that he could have recognized the presence of animal-headed gods, and the stylized representations of human figures that were conspicuously absent in the monolith inscriptions.

No, wait—there had been one recurring *motif* in most of the inscriptions. A little stick figure bearing what had looked like sheaves of wheat. That at least was Egyptian. But it was Assyrian, Babylonian, Trojan as well. In fact, there had been no ancient civilization in which that *motif* had not recurred on tomb-wall or temple engravings. But in going back over every visit he had ever made to a museum he was unable to recall having seen it so often repeated, amidst a small number of inscriptions that contained a great many other configurations that bore not the slightest resemblance to it.

It was as if the little stick figure had become an obsession and been turned into the only pictorial symbol worth recording—as if the written glyptographs were merely embellishments designed to shower lavish praise on it, or perhaps just to indicate the great awe that it inspired and the homage that should be rendered it.

The monoliths and the domed mountain were being swallowed up now by the darkness, were growing dimmer and dimmer. And suddenly even the last glimmer of half-light was gone, and the darkness became ink-black and impenetrable.

He could see nothing at all and he had the feeling that the ground on which he had been standing was dissolving beneath his feet and he was sinking down into an unfathomable gulf of emptiness. Sinking at first and then falling, his body becoming heavier, picking up speed as it plunged downward, moving with as great a velocity as a rock would have done if it had been hurled into the abyss from the top of the mountain. After that—there seemed to be nothing left to experience or remember.

CHAPTER NINE

Blakemore felt the tugging before he heard the far-off woman's voice pleading with him. He could tell that it was a pleading voice just by the way it sounded. The words meant nothing to him until the voice came much nearer and the tugging stopped, as if whoever had taken hold of his arm had decided that the words alone, if she whispered them right into his ear, would awaken him just as quickly.

"Dan, Dan—please. Open your eyes and look at me. You did a moment ago. Don't you remember?"

He couldn't remember. But if Helen said so it was probably true, because, unlike most women, when something that she might have to struggle to make him accept happened she saw no reason to keep it to herself.

The instant he opened his eyes and looked at her, precisely as she had urged him to do, everything came back —too fast for comfort. The snake bite, the cutting, her lips on his wounded heel, the stomach cramps and—the darting pains had been bad, bad. He had thought he was going to die. Why hadn't he?

She didn't give him much time to remember. She just bent and kissed him until he had to plead with her to stop, because there were things he had to know immediately.

Was the venom still winning? Had she come into the compartment to be with him when—

"Do you know how long you've slept?" she asked, which answered nothing, except that it did not seem exactly the kind of question a dying man would be likely to display the slightest interest in. Just the fact that she had asked it almost had to mean that his ability to sleep had seemed so encouraging a sign to her that she could hardly wait to tell him about it.

"No, I don't," he said. "I guess you'd better—"

"Just lean back now. Don't try to sit up too quickly," she cautioned, the instant he started to raise himself. "You've slept for almost a day and a half. Philip and I have been in and out at least fifty times, taking your temperature, feeling your pulse, watching the fever go down. You stopped tossing back and forth hours ago. Everything's fine now. At least, it should be. You haven't any temperature and you certainly recognized me quickly enough. Oh, I was scared for a minute. But the way you're talking now—"

"I haven't said much," Blakemore reminded her. "But I'm not disoriented, if that's what you mean. Mind's clear enough. But I haven't tried moving around yet. I don't know how weak I am."

"You may not be weak at all," she said. "But you'd better wait a few minutes before you try to move around. No setting up exercises, darling. Don't try to prove too much. It doesn't seem to have been a very poisonous snake."

"It was a deadly killer snake," Blakemore said, shaking his head. "All adders are. I was lucky, that's all. Every venomous snake bite doesn't inject into you the same amount of poison. There are lots and lots of recoveries, as Philip stressed. There were some lancinating pains in my arms and legs before I blacked out."

"Yes, I know. You kept groaning in your sleep for a long while. Poor darling—"

"I'm going to get up," Blakemore said, abruptly.

"No, don't. It would be a crazy thing to do—"

"I've got to find out. No sense in putting it off. If I get dizzy I can flop right back on the cot."

Before she could protest further Blakemore sat up and lowered his feet to the floor. In a moment he was not only on his feet but walking back and forth in front of the cot with his shoulders held straight.,

"It's incredible," he said. "I'm perfectly all right. Not a twinge. I've never felt better."

"That's because you've lead such a clean life. No smoking or drinking. It always helps."

"If I had to forego tobocco I'd let that snake bite me again." Blakemore said. "Liquor too, whenever a little of the watered-down stuff comes my way. If you mean, it's no longer possible for me or anyone else to be a heavy drinker—"

"You could smoke right now, if it would help," Helen said.

"It would," Blakemore confirmed. "Unfortunately, Roger borrowed my tobacco pouch. When there's something you'd *really* be grateful for it always seems to vanish."

"Yes, I've noticed it too. Whenever you say something like that I get a shock of recognition."

Suddenly all of the forced levity went out of Helen Blakemore's eyes. She grabbed hold of him, pressing her face hard against his chest, clinging to him with both arms. He could feel a wetness trickling down between his chest hairs. "If anything had happened to you—" She was mumbling the words and they sent a kind of vibration through his ribcage. "Dan, it would have happened to me too. Not in just the same way, but it would have happened. If any part of me stayed around for a-while, to walk about and talk to people, it would be just a shell."

"I don't think so, darling," Blakemore heard himself

replying as he stroked her hair. "Look, if everyone went on mourning the dead the world would turn into a big big funeral parlor. I'd want you to marry again and be happy."

"You don't really mean that."

"Well, I—"

"All right, it's what most people would expect you to say—even to think and feel. But you and I, Dan—we don't have to think in cliches. We don't have to at all, because what we have is very rare."

Suddenly she straightened and removed her head from his chest. He hadn't been mistaken about the trickling. Her eyes were so wet they looked like tiny lakes vertically suspended on opposite sides of her nose. The insane fear came upon him that all of the water might suddenly drain out of them, and he was quick to prevent that by flicking away the wetness, very gently, with his thumb. Instinctively she shut her eyes, enabling him to admire, for the ten-thousandth time, the veined delicacy of the lids.

She managed to smile. "Dan, if it would help you to smoke it will take me only a minute to get you that tobacco. You could get it yourself, but I'd like to be the one to tell Roger the good news. Philip too, of course."

"Well, all right," he said. "But don't be gone long and please come back alone. Not that their concern doesn't mean a lot to me. I probably owe my life to Philip's presence of mind. I was damned shaky, and if he hadn't applied the tourniquet fast—"

He looked down and stamped his bitten foot. "Circulation there seems to be okay now," he said. "When did Philip take the tourniquet off? Within forty-five minutes or so, I should imagine. I've heard it's a little risky to leave one on for more than half an hour.

"We both came back to see how you were after about twenty minutes," Helen said. "Philip felt it would take you that long at least to fall asleep, and that if you needed us you'd use the communicator, as he told you to do. You were asleep, but tossing about and groaning when we looked in on you. Philip loosened the knot a little and pulled out the wooden splinter he'd used to tighten it with. About an hour after that he removed the tourniquet completely."

"A risk in that too," Blakemore said. "But I guess he figured if gangrene set in I'd have no chance at all, and he had to balance one risk against another."

"Please don't," Helen said. "I'd rather not think about it. It's over and done with. I'll get you the tobacco."

Just before she passed out through the entrance panel directly opposite the cot he said again: "Come right back —alone. I just want to sit here quietly for about fifteen more minutes with my arm around you."

"I don't like tobacco smoke when it's swirling all around me, as I've told you again and again," she said. "But this time—it will be heavenly."

He sat down on the cot as soon as the panel glided shut, not because he'd been mistaken about how completely recovered he was, but simply because, after a moment of great uncertainty and strain, it was more natural to sit than to stand. Besides, he had nothing important to do until she got back and it was easier to just sit there with his hands on his knees and his eyes trained on the panel, waiting for it to glide open again.

The trouble was, it didn't open for so long a time that he got restless and stood up again. What could be keeping her? Both Faran and Roger were certain to be waiting impatiently for her to return with either good news or bad and could hardly have been far from the compartment. It surprised him a little that Faran had not been at Helen's side, that he had awakened to see only her face bending over him. But that could be put down

109

to her conviction that he would soon open his eyes and her determination to be alone with him when it happened.

But surely Faran, Gilda and Roger were just outside, probably at the end of the passageway. Why then was it taking her so long to secure his tobacco pouch from Roger?

The minutes seemed to be lengthening out, to be turning into hours. Possibly not more than five minutes had passed, but how could he be sure of that? He was losing all track of the time. Besides, five minutes were three minutes too many. He was sorry now he'd said anything about the tobacco. It wasn't all that important.

He suddenly realized he was making too much out of it. There was nothing to stop him from going in search of her. He owed that to Faran anyway, even if Helen had already told him. "See, here I am, as well as ever. Helen and I will not soon forget what you did for us. Now she and I are going to relax for a while. We'll put a 'do not disturb' sign on the panel and I'll pack some of that stringy, stale tobacco into my pipe that Roger doesn't seem to appreciate and light up. Come next Thursday, we'll all go outside and have a picnic in the cornbrake. No, the big, exotic, year 500,057-type flower garden. There are no stinging vines out there, or cannibal plants or anything like that, as far as I've been able to determine. Adders? Oh, a few, of course—Mamba-green and very beautiful, at least in coloration. But we won't let them scare us, will we? If one of them should bite us a tourniquet and a little extra attention to the wound will fix us up fine and dandy. We'll be new men and women—"

It was a new man who crossed to the panel, activated the opening mechanism and waited for it to glide open —a man quite different from the one Blakemore had felt himself to be when his anxiety had been getting out of hand a few seconds earlier. What he'd needed most of all, he now realized, was a strong incentive to stride about confidently outside of just one narrow compartment. It was the best and quickest way of making absolutely sure that all of his strength had come back.

The instant he emerged into the passageway all of his anxiety threatened to return. It wasn't so much that the passageway was deserted. Faran and the others could easily be waiting a little farther away. It was the stillness. Not a whisper of sound anywhere, nothing that remotely resembled a far-off murmur of voices.

It was the kind of stillness that could make you feel that you were standing in a vacuum, with no medium that could carry sound waves to your ears even if they had been present immediately outside the vacuum. It was even worse than that. It was as if the entire machine had become a vacuum, had turned into the exact opposite of an echoing chamber, with all sound sucked away into emptiness.

Always before there had been sounds of one sort or another. Even walls of solid metal made sounds continuously, very tiny stress signals that you couldn't actually hear but that you somehow remained unconsciously aware of. The inaudible creaking of the inanimate. You were most aware of it in the control compartment, with its intricate tiers of machinery. No one could stand close to a big, silent computer, even when it wasn't cerebrating and remain unaware of it. It didn't have to be clicking out punched tapes. Just its sheer mechanical weariness after that kind of toil could make it give off fatigue signals. Machines, particularly complex ones, never stopped complaining and the metal walls of a machine that had traveled thousands of years into the future should have had more to complain about than the most weary of giant computers.

There was one thing, Blakemore knew, that he must do immediately. Such thoughts were wild indeed, and although he could not deny that there was some truth in them, he must stop blowing it up in that way. There was just a kind of unnatural stillness around him, period. He had experienced the same feeling before, many times, and even though it had seldom been quite as pronounced as now it could still turn out to have been a delusion.

Another thing he must do was refuse to take seriously, even for the space of a skipped heartbeat, the even more alarming thought that something had hapened to Helen and the others and he was alone in the machine. That, too, could have created a stillness, for the absence of a living presence that you've taken for granted, that you've visualized as still close at hand, could make you feel more totally cut off from the stir of life than a long period of solitude to which you'd become accustomed. The harder to believe, the more incredible such an unexpected stillness seemed, the more acute your awareness of it became.

Just the fact that he could have been standing straighter, that he was letting it get to him to such an extent that he was losing confidence in the complete return of his strength, made him square his shoulders and advance in quick strides to the end of the passageway.

He passed around the first turn and was half-way down the equally deserted passageway that branched off from it when he ran into Roger.

The passageway had been deserted when he'd made the turn, because at that moment Roger had no more than started to come in view around the sharp-angled wall where the passageway branched for the second time.

Roger had covered the intervening distance in a forward lurch that was half a stagger and half a leap, so quickly that he smashed into Blakemore before the latter could hurl himself to one side.

He would have gone right on past if Blakemore hadn't recovered his balance, and flung his arms around him, not in a warm comradely embrace, but with the embat-

112

tled anger of a man who refuses to be almost knocked off his feet by anyone, friend or foe, without demanding and getting an explanation.

Roger's face had the half-insane, wildly twitching look of a man goaded beyond endurance by something that he has seen or heard or endured as a result of atrocious physical violence.

But somehow, just the fact that it was Blakemore who was holding fast to him and not an extension of some unimaginable horror pursuing him along the corridor emabled him to conquer—or hold in abeyance—enough of his fright to make what came from his lips intelligible.

"Malador got away! I'm going after him. Dan, *don't try to stop me*. If you do, I'll have to make you let go of me. I'm bigger, stronger than you are—"

"Now look—" Blakemore flared. "If you think—"

"Oh, for God's sake, can't you realize that's not a boast or anything. I just happen to be built that way. You know I can do it. And I'll have to—if you make me."

There was a strange look in Tyson's eyes. Blakemore had seen that look before. It was that of a man who felt guilty right down to his soles, shaken to the depths by something he'd done or said. But Blakemore had the feeling that it had nothing to do with what Roger had *just* said and his curiosity overcame his anger.

"All right," he said. "If you want to get yourself killed I can't stop you. Just tell me one thing—and I'll step aside and let you do that. Where is Helen? Is she all right? If she'd been harmed I'll go with you—even if a midget doesn't pack much of a punch."

"Dan, I told you I didn't mean it that way. Helen's all right. So is Gilda."

"And Faran?"

"He's paralyzed. But it will wear off. He tried to stop Malador by struggling with him, and that skeleton ape trained the—the trident on him. Helen and Gilda are

113

with him. I'm sure he'll come out of it. Malador's still grateful to him, I think—wouldn't want to kill him. It's you he wants to kill."

"I see. The gut-level hatred is still there. He had the best chance he'll ever get. What didn't he take it?"

"He thought he had—*yesterday*. He thought you were dying—or dead. You can't exact vengeance on the dead. Good God, that's what Faran's always saying. Well —it's true."

It suddenly seemed to Blakemore that he might be losing his mind. He tightened his grip on Tyson's shoulders, shook him. "You've got to help me get this straight. Then I'll let you go. How could he have tried to kill me? The snake tried and almost succeeded. But what had Malador to do with—"

"Everything," Tyson said. "He made you step on that snake, with his mind. He knew it was there. He's—well, clairvoyant. He has hypnotic powers as well—extra-sensory hypnotic powers."

"I can't believe that. Malador—"

"Dan, listen to me," Tyson pleaded. "He made me let him out of the compartment. He didn't have to use the trident, he just told me to let him out and I did. And he came walking right out with the trident. Possibly he couldn't have done that earlier. All I can be sure of is that he tried and succeeded once before in forcing me to —to obey him. The word sticks in my mouth but I might as well say it. I went into the instrument compartment and made changes on three of the dials. That's why the machine went careening through Time. That's why we're here."

"He forced you to— You mean, you were under an hypnotic spell?"

Tyson nodded. "I was in a trance—both times. The first time it was so deep I came out of it without knowing what I had done. This time I knew exactly what I was doing, what was going on around me. But I still had to obey him. Maybe he was working up to that, bending all his efforts toward making me let him out. I couldn't lift a hand to help Philip when he was struggling with him. But I could see, I knew. The hypnosis must have been stronger in one way, lighter in another. That could happen—"

"But how could you have known what you did when you were in the first trance?"

"I put two and two together. I can't be absolutely sure, of course. But doesn't it seem logical it must have happened that way? Changes were made in the dials. And no living hand beside my own could have made them. I was alone in the instrument compartment when you arrived with Faran, and your wife. Gilda was in her own compartment at the opposite end of the machine."

Tyson's voice changed, became more urgently pleading, almost stricken in its appeal. "Let go of me, Dan. Don't force me to lash out at you. I'd win, you know, and that's still not a boast. I've got to go after him and bring him back."

"In God's name, why?" Blakemore demanded. "If he can make me step on a poisonous snake and force you to obey an hypnotic command, bringing him back could be suicidal. He has the trident-shaped weapon to fall back on if he can't repeat what he did to you. What chance would you have? Unarmed as you are—"

Tyson shook his head. "I'm not quite that much of a fool. He didn't take the other weapon—the death-dealing one—with him. Philip has made access to it very difficult, and he forgot to make me bring it to him. I'm on my way to get it now."

"He didn't forget. I'm sure of that. If what you say about him is true he has too many other strings to his bow to be concerned about your going in pursuit of him. I can't imagine just why he wanted to escape, if he thought I was dead and he could have killed you and

Helen. I can understand his wanting to spare Faran and his daughter out of gratitude, but otherwise—"

"There must have been some slipup—a kind of blind spot in his thinking—or he *would* have made me get the more powerful weapon," Tyson said. "So what I said about forgetting still goes. He'll certainly need that weapon *out there*."

"I know," Blakemore conceded. "And that's our best hope. Don't you see? Let him stay out there. He'll be a twenty-second century man in an age as unknown to him as it is to us. Just as hazardous an age, with just as many unexplored pitfalls—"

"No," Tyson said, shaking his head. "I can't see myself doing that. We don't know what he may be up to. Extrasensory hypnosis is something special. It can apparently operate from a distance. He didn't have to look at me or talk to me. He just sat quietly inside the compartment and forced me to do his bidding. The first time, I mean. And even the second time to start with.

"All hypnosis is supposed to be self-hypnosis," he went on after a pause. "You look into the hypnotist's eyes or a bright light and what you actually do is send yourself into a trance. A kind of hysteria sweeps over you. Then, of course, you start obeying the hypnotist's spoken commands. You either do what he commands immediately or carry out, on awakening, the post-hypnotic suggestion which he has implanted in your mind. But when you can't see or hear the hypnotist at all—"

Tyson began to tremble a little under Blakemore's still firm grip on his shoulders. "You've got to let go of me. He's got to be brought back. I don't care how great the risk may be."

"There's something you forgot," Blakemore said. "If what you say is true—it does violence to everything that has always been known about hypnosis. You're not supposed to be able to make a hypnotized man do anything

116

that outrages his moral sense—or goes against the grain in some other way. A *very slight* resistance can be overcome by persuasion sometimes, but it takes great skill. That's what makes me doubt that Malador could have made you—"

"Are you suggesting that I *wanted* to make the machine go out of control? Or make sure that snake would bite you—or even to let Malador out of the compartment, so that he could risk his life, as you've said, in an unknown world? Because if you are—"

"You might have unconsciously wanted to do the last," Blakemore said. "But let's put it this way. You may have had an unconscious fear, a constant dread, that the machine might go out of control in just this way—on Philip's next journey. And Malador may have exercised just enough extrasensory influence over you to make you *act out* what you feared in a trance-like state. You would not want it to happen but your fear that it might happen would cause you to make it happen. It's like—well, you're standing on a high cliff in a dream and have an uncontrollable impulse to hurl yourself to the rocks far below. And not always in a dream."

"And would that explain how Malador made you step on the snake. Did I dread that, too?"

"I'm not sure," Blakemore said. "You may have actually dreaded something of the sort, when you saw me descend into that boggy flower garden, amidst all those gigantic fronds."

"But that would have to mean that I, and not Malador, was in extrasensory-contact with your mind," Tyson said. "It makes no sense at all."

"It could have been a three-way communication," Blakemore said. "But you're right. It strains credulity. I'm just trying to make you see that Malador may not be quite as dangerous to us *out there* as you seem to feel. There may be other ways of explaining what happened.

He may be—he probably is—clairvoyant. And he can send you into a kind of trance—an extrasensory trance. But that may be the whole of it."

"For the last time," Tyson said, warningly. "Will you let go of me. I'm going after him."

Blakemore looked at him steadily for a moment. "Just before you crashed into me I got a good look at your face," he said. "You seemed less to be going in pursuit of Malador than fleeing from something behind you. It was as if you were being pursued yourself, by the Furies. We might as well keep it Aeschylean, since that trident made you wonder how Poseidon would have looked walking back and forth on a Connecticut beach. Could it have been a feeling of guilt you were fleeing from, Roger? Is that why you're so set on risking *your* life *out there*? As a way of redeeming what you could not forgive yourself for having done? If so—I urge you to forget it. You have no guilt to live down. It could have happened to me, to Philip—to anyone."

"Damn you!" Tyson flared. "When you feel there's no time to be lost you can seem to be running from something when everything that matters is straight ahead of you. Quit trying to head-shrink me—"

Suddenly he stopped being angry. Blakemore could see what an effort it cost him and the way he'd always felt about Tyson—it had been shaken for a moment—came back.

"I'm sorry," Tyson said. "I know you were just trying to make me feel better about what happened. Of course I feel guilty. I should. You don't know—"

"I think I do," Blakemore said. "And I still say—forget it."

"I can't. But there's more to it than just my being unable to forgive myself. Malador should be back here with us, with all of us guarding him. If he's where he was again, without that trident and— Oh, hell, don't you see? He'd have a hard time making all of us go into a trance.

118

You could keep me bound hand and foot, if necessary."

"What you mean is—there are some people who can't be hypnotized, even when it isn't extrasensory. That's true, of course. It has failed with me every time it's been tried. I'm not boasting, mind you—I was just built that way."

"All right, I deserved that."

"I can't quite believe that he has the power to put you into a trance-like state at any time, in any place," Blakemore went on quickly. "Or that it actually was extrasensory hypnosis, despite the fact that you let him out. As for the snake, I could have stepped on it without outside help. But let's say you're right—and you may well be. If he has that power over you—or even a lesser power—how can you hope to bring him back, no matter how formidably armed you may be."

"I can try," Tyson said.

"No, you're not going to even try," Blakemore said. "I won't let you."

"You won't let—"

"If anyone goes outside with that weapon it will be me," Blakemore said. "And I'll have to think about it, because I'm not at all sure we're not better off with Malador stepping on poisonous snakes or running a constant risk of getting himself killed in some other way. It's a harsh thing to have to say, but we might be better off if we never set eyes on him again."

All of Tyson's anger came back.

"That's beautiful, Dan *You're* going to stop *me*. I've got fifty pounds advantage on you in weight alone. I'm close to a foot taller and I've got a much longer reach. Let go of me, Dan. I wasn't joking before, but now I'm twice as serious."

"Thanks for not mentioning the edge you have on me in years," Blakemore said. "Some men start falling apart when they pass the thirty mark."

"Don't make me do that. I could, you know, because

if you were Philip's age I'd still have to flatten you out if you gave me no choice. That's how set I am on going after him."

"All right," Blakemore said. "Try to break loose."

Tyson took a quick step backwards, almost wrenching his shoulders free and carrying Blakemore with him.

Blakemore made just three movements in all. The first was an upward chopping one, the second a downward chopping one and the third a kind of twisting that ended in a somersaulting toss. They were executed as swiftly as a magician's pass.

Tyson looked up at him from the floor, his sprawled out body mirrored by its gleaming metal surface with only a few slight distortions here and there. The actual physical distortion which the first movement had brought about—a slight, reddish swelling in the region of his jaw—did not show in the mirrored image.

For a moment Tyson said nothing at all—just lay where he had fallen with a look of stark incredulity in his eyes. Then, abruptly, he began to laugh.

Blakemore found himself laughing as well.

Quickly Tyson got to his feet, still laughing and brushing invisible dust particles from his clothes, as if he'd forgotten that a dustless metal floor was quite different from a Connecticut beach with its above-tide surface of blowing sand.

"I've always felt that a man who can't admit defeat and take it in stride isn't worth a damn," he said. "I'm not sure I'd say that, though, if I could duplicate what you just did."

"I'd be glad to show you exactly how it was done," Blakemore said. "I'm sure you could master it in two easy lessons. It took me much longer."

"No thank you," Tyson said. "If there was someone else here you could demonstrate it on I might take you up on it. But since it would have to be me—"

"Some other time then."

"Yes, that suits me fine. You must think I'm crazy, but I swear to you it wasn't being floored like that that made me change my mind. Oh, I suppose it did, in a way, because it jolted me up enough to make what you last said really register. You said you couldn't be hypnotized. I heard it all right, when you said it, but the implications didn't really sink in until I hit the floor. You're naturally the man to go, and of course I'll go with you, if you'll let me. And thinking it over before you decide is all right with me too. You could be right, we may be safer with Malador outside. It might be wise for both of us to do a little more thinking all along the line."

"I should have done more right after I grabbed hold of you," Blakemore said. "I had to know why you'd slammed into me and when you told me you'd let Malador out in a trance and were going after him, I felt I had to drum some sense into you at any cost. But if I'd known it would take so long I'd have let you go, and gotten to Philip. Just the fact that Helen and Gilda are with him doesn't mean the paralysis will wear off."

"I'm sure it will. It probably has by now."

"Just what makes you so sure?"

"I told you. I know I can trust the way I feel about Malador not wanting to harm Philip or Gilda in a serious way. I should have stayed with him. But I lost my head. All I could think of was getting the weapon and over-taking Malador before he could thrash his way out of the vegetation it took you more than five minutes to cross. He's probably just about reaching the end of it—"

"Let's hope that Philip isn't thrashing about in a darkness that's not going to lift," Blakemore said. "Come on, we've got to find out."

They were at the end of the passageway and turning into a wider one when Tyson said, "By taking as long as you did to drum some sense into me you probably saved my life. Just thought I'd mention it, for whatever it may be worth."

CHAPTER TEN

Faran was sitting on the floor a few feet to the right of the viewing window, with his legs drawn up and his shoulders slightly slumped. He was leaning back against the wall and made no attempt to rise when Blakemore and Tyson entered the compartment. Neither did Gilda, who was kneeling at his side and pressing a wet cloth to his brow.

Helen Blakemore had been kneeling also, but she got up quickly and darted to her husband's side.

"He's all right now," she said. "But we were terrible frightened at first. Did Roger tell you what happened? He must have or you wouldn't be together."

"He told me," Blakemore said, nodding. "When you didn't come back I was afraid—well, I didn't think you'd been detained by anything as serious as this. But I had the feeling something unusual had happened."

"It was unusual, all right," Faran said. His voice was surprisingly firm and his eyes were not those of a man who has any doubt as to his ability to think clearly and forcefully.

Suddenly he was looking at Tyson, almost accusingly.

"I caught only a brief glimpse of you when I was struggling with him," he said. "You seemed to be just standing back against the wall, doing nothing to help me. You could have tried to knock him down while his back was turned to you and just before he trained that weapon on me. But I'm not reproaching you, Roger. Don't misunderstand me. I'm just puzzled. You could have been too startled to think clearly. How do you suppose he got out? Have you any idea?"

"I have a very good idea, unfortunately," Tyson said. "I let him out."

"You did *what?*"

Blakemore laid a firm hand on Tyson's arm. "You'd better let me tell him, Roger."

"Tell me what?" Faran demanded. "After what he just said—if there is any talking to be done—"

Blakemore crossed to where Faran was sitting and knelt with his left leg bent and his right knee resting on the floor. He had to lower his head a little more to bring it on a level with Faran's ear. Faran removed the damp cloth from his forehead and returned it to his daughter, who was still on her knees directly across from Blakemore and seemed reluctant to rise.

"I don't need this now," he said. "Get up, Gilda. Dan has something to tell me you may not want to hear."

"If Roger let Malador out," Gilda said, "I'm sure it's not anything I'd prefer not to know about. Something must have happened that gave him no choice."

"I did have no choice, darling," Tyson said. "But somehow it doesn't quite seem to excuse what I was forced to do. Dan thinks I must be off my rocker to feel that way. I realize that it makes no sense, but I've got to be honest about it. Perhaps if I'd put up more of an inner struggle—"

"This is getting us nowhere," Faran said. "All right, Dan. Roger opened the panel and let Malador out. He's confessed to that. And what he just said makes it sound like something you're going to have a great deal of difficulty explaining away. But I want to hear all of it. Then I'll decide for myself."

Blakemore told him, leaving nothing out.

For a moment Faran remained silent, his lips set in tight lines. Then he said: "What I'm going to say may surprise you. I don't share a single one of your doubts, Dan. You've tried to rationalize a part of it, have put a remarkably ingenious, psychologically adroit interpretation on what you think may have happened. No doubt you've succeeded—or almost succeeded—in convincing Roger that, while Malador may be clairvoyant and possess ESP gifts that are unusual in other respects he couldn't possibly hypnotize anyone, sight unseen, and enforce absolute, unquestioning obedience to his every command. Or compel you to step on a poisonous reptile and perhaps even draw that reptile toward you with a deliberate effort of will, extrasensorily enforced.

Faran's expression became grave. "I think he may be able to do more than that. I think he may possess the power to move and shake."

"The power to—move and shake?"

Faran nodded. "Yes, to move objects at a distance, to lift them into the air and send them whirling about. Perhaps even to teleport a huge block of stone over a considerable distance. Many such occurrences have been recorded. It's called *psychokinesis*."

"No, Philip!" Helen Blakemore heard herself protesting. "You can't really believe that."

"I think it's distinctly possible," Faran said. "I don't think it's too likely. I'm more inclined to believe that what Roger told Dan he was almost sure of comes closer to the truth—that Malador had to *work up* to actually getting Roger to set him free—that about all he could do at first was hypnotize Roger in a superficial way and compel him to make those changes in the dials. Otherwise he would have escaped before this."

"But what makes you so—" It was seldom that Blakemore was at a loss for words, but for an instant he felt as if a clamp had tightened around his tongue.

Faran seemed to guess what he'd started to ask, for there was a look of complete understanding in his eyes. "You're naturally wondering why I seem so sure that Malador is more than just clairvoyant. I'm basing it on what happened to Roger, and something else of greater importance.

"I wouldn't go so far to say that I'm a hundred percent sure. There is the *barest* possibility that you may be right, Dan—that he didn't actually hypnotize Roger but simply made him more responsive to unconscious impulses already present in his mind. Guided and directed Roger's thoughts, in other words, so that the acts he performed were brought about by his own unconscious fears.

"But what makes me feel that he compelled Roger to obey him in a more direct and forceful way is—well, everything that we know about the hidden powers of the mind. It is only in the East that those powers have been developed to their full potential across the centuries. The evidence of that is overwhelming. You'd have to have a gigantic blind spot to deny it.

"The Hindu rope trick. Can anyone in his right mind believe that it starts and ends with that—that for centuries Eastern seers and so-called 'holy men' have not been performing miracles of teleportation, blind sight, suspended animation, clairvoyance that doesn't just come in brief flashes but illuminates vast areas of experience that the occidental world knows very little about."

"But Malador did not come from the East," Blakemore heard himself protesting.

"How do you know? Actually he never set foot in the Orient. He comes from Western Europe, from a region bordering on the Mediterranean which, in the twenty-second century, is no longer a part of France. But just the fact that you didn't even ask me whether he came from the East or West should help you to understand why I feel as I do about him."

"I'm afraid I don't understand—"

"Why didn't you ask me? It is the first question you should have asked, because it is the most natural thing in the world for a man who has traveled in time to draw a map for you. The region's geographical features—its precise locality—should have aroused your curiosity beyond anything else. But you didn't even ask. Shall I tell you why?"

"If it will help me to understand, I guess you'd better. But it's all very strange. I had the feeling I didn't have to ask—that I *knew.*"

"You thought you knew—and you were not greatly mistaken. Only slightly so. You thought he must come from a country very much like India, where the spectre of starvation can turn the thoughts of men inward as it has never done in the West, despite the blight, despite everything.

"When I described that age to you there came into your mind a picture of thousands of emaciated men and women, half-naked, despairing, seeking escape from their wretchedness by the kind of self-imposed and tormented introspection that has actually, in India as we've known it across the centuries, increased the hidden powers of the mind.

"Contemplation, constant brooding, a summoning of an inner strength to resist an environmental deprivation that would otherwise be unbearable. The weakest slew or were slain in a desperate struggle to avoid starvation. Others, the strongest, managed to survive with little or no food and turned into gaunt skeletons like Malador. It happened in India centuries ago and in the twentieth century, too, of course and it could happen anywhere on earth in the twenty-second century, because the world I visited was like that everywhere.

"There must be many Maladors in the twenty-second century. Emaciated skeletons with the mind's powers so highly developed as to seem almost limitless.

126

"We thought Malador was no different from all of the others who begged us to save them, often falling to their knees, sobbing and pleading.

"But I'm almost sure now that he was one of the strong ones, with the power, as I've said, to move and shake. That does not mean that he would not have welcomed food as well. Starvation or near-starvation is never pleasant. And if he was one of the strong ones, Dan, his hatred of you could be just as all-consuming. The only difference would be—his inner strength would make him a hundred times more dangerous, a hundred times more determined to exact retribution for the torment that he has endured."

"What you are really saying is that developing the hidden powers of the mind does not always turn men and women into saints," Helen Blakemore said.

"Exactly," Faran said. "I'm feeling much better now, but not because of that. I think I can get up without having the compartment start pinwheeling the way it did a moment ago."

"All right, let's try it," Blakemore said. He took firm hold of Faran's arm, but when Tyson started forward Gilda gestured him back. "Dad doesn't need all that help, Roger," she said. "Dan and I will take care of it."

It seemed a surprising thing for her to have said, and for the barest instant there flashed across Blakemore's mind a thought that might have thrilled him in some other age as remote in Time, long ago or far away and if the only woman more important to him than a thousand others combined could have been had not come into his life at all.

It was almost as if Gilda, despite herself, could not quite forgive Roger for what he had done and was letting him think that he had a rival she was experiencing no need to forgive at all.

It was a mad thought and the instant Faran was on his feet Blakemore saw how mistaken he had been, for she darted instantly to Roger's side, linked her arm with his, and kissed him firmly on the cheek.

"I was ready to believe, when the paralysis started to wear off, that Malador had actually borrowed that weapon from Poseidon in some way," Faran said, with a twisted smile. "A god of the sea must have possessed hidden powers of the mind as well—quite extraordinary ones, if Homer was not a bald-faced liar. Who knows? There may have been a man like Malador once in the Aegean world whom the Greeks later deified."

"A god of storm and shipwreck," Blakemore said. "Yes, I can well believe it."

"He probably hated both the land itself and all landsmen," Gilda said. "It makes sense. He may have been a lean and hungry god, and when he saw a field of golden wheat he shook his trident in rage, a storm arose and the land became flooded.

"If a man like Dan had grown that wheat I'm sure Homer would not have let it be forgotten," Faran said.

"Perhaps he didn't," Blakemore said. "He may have turned me into the Cyclops. One-eyed and short-sighted. Polyphemus was the wrong kind of landsman."

"*Far-sighted*, you mean," Faran said. "Your wheat built the cities we saw. No short-sighted Cyclops could have done that. Besides, you've nothing in common with a Cyclops, apart from being a giant."

Before Blakemore could comment on the absurdity of that the compartment did what Faran had feared it might —for him at least. It began to pinwheel.

CHAPTER ELEVEN

It was a swaying as well as a pinwheeling, a movement of the entire compartment that was not unlike the rising and falling movements of a ship at sea, riding the crest of a high wave and then descending into the trough. It lacked the violence, the swift, erratic tossing about of a ship caught in a gale. But it was not on that account less terrifying, for the floor tilted at a precarious angle before it righted itself again, threatening to hurl the occupants to the floor.

Only Faran did not become wildly alarmed. The look on his face was merely one of chagrin, and he immediately sat down again, clearly thinking that it was a wave of dizziness sweeping over him that was causing the compartment to sway and spin about.

Then, abruptly, the vexation vanished from his eyes and was replaced by as great a look of fear as he had worn when he had first discovered that the dials had shifted about and the machine could not be stopped from careening through Time, completely out of control.

Blakemore's concern, on seeing him descend to the floor, had prevented him from keeping as well-balanced as the others, and he was hurled to his knees just as Faran arose, with Gilda's screams echoing in his ears. Helen simply drew in her breath but so sharply that he was sure he would have heard the sound as she had been three or four feet away instead of almost at his side.

She was even closer to him when he regained his feet, for an increase in the swaying was forcing her to cling to him for support.

All at once the swaying stopped and the compartment became totally still again. But the viewing window had become enveloped, on its outer surface, in what looked for an instant like a solid sheet of flame.

Then there were flames inside the compartment as well, dancing on the walls, streaming across the floor in widening banners that wrapped themselves around Tyson and Gilda, blotting them from view, and then turned into a thin dragon's tongue spitting fire.

The dragon's tongue was forked as well, and one fiery filament ascended and coiled around Faran's head, and shoulders. His hair seemed to catch fire. Helen screamed as Gilda had done, and went limp in her husband's arms.

Blakemore was retreating with her toward the opposite wall when all of the flames expired. No one appeared to have been harmed. Tyson and Gilda could not have looked more shaken and their lips were drained of all color. But their clothes had not caught fire and their arms and faces were not scorched. Neither had Faran's hair been burned away. It had, in fact, not been burned at all.

Blakemore could only hope that the seemingly heatless flames had not inflicted injuries which were invisible and might be slow to heal. But the look which Faran was exchanging with him was not that of a man who had been wounded in his mind, at least not grievously, and Tyson and Gilda were raising and lowering their arms and looking down over themselves with considerably less fear in their eyes, although it was far from an absence of fear.

Only Helen Blakemore remained limp and unstirring in her husband's arms. He looked at Faran almost accusingly as he lowered her to the floor. "She fainted when she saw the flames swirl up over your head," he said. "I'll try chaffing her wrists. I hope it helps."

"Don't do anything," Faran said. "Just ease her gently down, and let her recover by herself. She's going to be all right."

He swung about and moved unsteadily toward the viewing window, and for an instant Blakemore was angered by what he mistook for a lack of concern. Then he saw that there was still a brightness beyond the pane. It had ceased to look like a solid sheet of flame, but there was nothing reassuring about that. The glare was less bright but Blakemore knew from experience, having once nearly lost his life in trying to put out a fire, that high-leaping flames that darted in all directions could be more difficult to bring under control than just one steady blaze.

He was on his knees at his wife's side, chaffing her wrists despite what Faran had said and pleading with her to open her eyes when Tyson's voice came to his ears. He was pleading with Gilda in much the same way, except that he wasn't trying to awaken her from a dead faint but simply doing his best to calm her down.

"The swaying is gone and the flames are gone and nothing more may happen—at least for awhile. If it's Malador and that's the best he can do— Don't you realize what it means? He's shot his belt and failed."

"I'm terribly frightened, Roger," Gilda's voice was barely audible, a kind of half-whisper, choked, despairing. "Those were real flames, not just reflections of light. You can always tell."

"Not always, no. We weren't burned. There was no heat."

"But I *felt* them, swirling around me. There was a slight heat. Please, Roger—don't deny it. You know it's true. The next time—"

"The flames outside are real enough!" Faran's voice

131

cut in sharply. "The vegetation is burning. And the machine was moved. Not much, but a little. There's no question about it—"

"Dad, how do you know?"

"The flowering plants—the biggest ones—aren't as close as they were. The whole alignment has changed. The glare makes them stand out."

"Are you sure?" It was Roger's voice again.

"Yes . . . yes. I can tell."

Blakemore neither looked toward the viewing window nor across the compartment toward Tyson and Gilda. He had not removed his eyes from his wife's face, nor his hands from her wrists. He was glad that he hadn't, for she was stirring now and the color had come back into her face.

Suddenly she opened her eyes and looked up at him. He was almost sure he knew, from the way her pupils quivered and widened, the exact moment when she remembered what had caused her to faint.

In a moment she was sitting up, her fingers biting into his wrists.

"Stay steady, darling," he pleaded. "Philip's all right. So are Roger and Gilda."

"But I'm not. I've never had so terrible a shock. There's a quivering inside me and I—I can't make it stop. How can Philip be all right? His head was ablaze."

"I tell you, he is. There were no burns."

"I don't see him. Where—"

"I'm right here," Faran said, having crossed so quickly from the viewing window to where she was sitting that he was standing directly behind her with his hand on her shoulder before Blakemore's eyes could sweep the compartment.

"We're still in danger," he said, "because the vegetation outside is burning and the machine is right in the midst of the flames. The flames outside may be hot

132

enough to damage the machine. I'm just guessing, of course, but I think when the flames penetrate a thick metal barrier they lose most of their heat. It's as if a harmless beam of light were swirling over us, except that it isn't quite like a harmless light beam in its fieriness, the way it singled us out and wrapped itself around us."

"I should think it would have to be an invisible heat ray, infra-red or some other ray situated below the red end of the visible spectrum to penetrate a metal barrier," Blakemore said. "It would have to be hot and invisible, not visible and without heat."

"It would have to be, of course," Faran said. "There's only one thing wrong with that. What it would have to be it isn't."

"But how can visible light penetrate an opaque metal barrier?" Blakemore persisted.

"I don't know," Faran said. "Do you?"

"A moment ago you were talking as if you did know," Blakemore couldn't help saying. "You based it on the educated guess that Malador knew exactly how to enlarge on the East Indian rope trick. I still don't quite share that point of view, but since you and Roger seem to think there's invisible writing on every folded-back part of the universe—what's so strange about it? If you're right, I mean."

Before Faran could say anything in reply Roger's voice caused him to swing about and postpone, for an instant, helping his wife to get up. Both Tyson and Gilda had managed to cross the compartment and were blocking off the light from the viewing window.

"Whatever you may believe, Dan," Roger said, moving a step closer. "We've got to do something about it. If Malador could move the machine, what that light failed to do is of no importance. It can only mean we're completely at his mercy, until he's—well, until he's stopped. There may be only one way of stopping him, and I don't think we should go on refusing to face it. I think you know what that way is, Dan. He's forfeited all claims to survival."

"Oh, hell," Blakemore heard himself saying. "What makes you think I'd draw back from that? If I was sure it was his life or ours I'd blast him down at the first opportunity, and that's entirely apart from the way he feels about me. But two things stand in the way. One—I'm still far from sure you and Philip are right about him. Moving the machine would take more doing than just lifting up a big boulder, say, and teleporting it a short distance. *Psychokinesis* may be a paranormal possibility. How should I know? I'm not enough of an expert to know what the hidden powers of the mind can accomplish, in India or elsewhere. But there's one thing I can't buy. That inside man's fragile cerebral cortex— it's like a blob of jelly—there's enough hidden power to move the machine. In a small way, it would be like moving a mountain.

"Two—" Blakemore went on, after a pause. "I don't think we could train a weapon on him—any kind of weapon—and blast him down in time to prevent him from stopping us. I'll concede you and Philip that much. He'd find some way of stopping us."

"He's right, Roger," Faran said. "I don't think I could operate the weapon he turned against Dan—and I doubt if you could. You were watching him closely on the beach when he started to bring down that gull. But he didn't complete the demonstration."

"I'm sure I can operate it," Tyson said. "But there's something Dan told me that would enable us to go after him with a much better chance of succeeding. *Dan can't be hypnotized.*"

Faran straightened and looked at Dan steadily for an instant. "Is that true?" he asked.

"I've encouraged a few hypnotists, exceptionally gifted ones, to try it—just out of curiosity," Blakemore told him. "It has never worked. It doesn't have to mean I'm particularly strong-willed. I didn't put up too much resistance—once or twice or none at all. That would have spoiled the experiment. Hypnosis just doesn't seem to work with some people."

"Extrasensory hypnosis—sight unseen, as Roger has stressed—might be different," Faran said. "I don't like that term. It's basically meaningless. But something of the sort undoubtedly exists and has been often practiced."

He hesitated, then said: "Still, still, it could change everything. If you can't be hypnotized in the usual way Malador might well be unable to get through to you. It would provide an added protection and if Roger is really convinced he can operate the weapon—"

He broke off abruptly, stood up and walked to the window. It gave Blakemore an opportunity, while he remained staring out, to help his wife to her feet. Up to that moment both she and Gilda had remained silent.

But now there was a fear in Helen's eyes that was exactly like the look that had come into them just before she had fainted, and her voice could not have been more chillingly close to desperation if it had been a voice from the tomb.

"You're not going to leave the machine. I won't let you. If you do—I'll find some way of not being here when you come back."

"Roger's not going outside either," Gilda said. "He's lying to you about the weapon. He told me he was far from sure he could operate it."

"I'm not the one who's lying," Roger said. But I can forgive you for that, darling, because I know why you—"

Faran's voice from the window prevented him from going on. Faran spoke without turning. "I think the fire's dying down a little," he said. "Since there's nothing out there that could stop a blaze like that in an ordinary way

Malador may want the flames to go out. About a third of the vegetation is seared, but it has stopped shriveling and blackening over a wide area."

"Between us we should be able to operate the weapon," Blakemore said, not wanting his wife to repeat what she had said, but fearing that she would. "I've always been rather—well, good with guns."

Before Helen could grasp the enormity of what he had said Faran turned from the window and spoke again.

"We'll have to wait, of course, until there are no more flames. The fire could blaze up again and get worse. It's still spreading a little here and there. But I've a feeling it's going to burn itself out—"

"Dad, don't you realize what that could mean?" Gilda almost screamed the words. "Malador may *want* Roger and Dan to go outside. He may be waiting for them to come out and get themselves killed. Maybe he found he couldn't move the machine enough to wreck it. He may have tried and failed. So he set that fire to bring Dan out. He must hate Roger too, now, because of what happened on the beach. But he needed him, right up to the last moment and after that—well, killing him may have seemed unimportant to him, not worth bothering about. But if he goes out with Dan—"

"We all know it's Dan he hates the most," Faran said. "That's why he must do the deciding."

He looked directly at Blakemore. "Gilda may be right," he said. "You may be walking into a trap that Malador has set for you. But before you decide, there are one or two things I think you should know. They have to do with how I feel about it. Malador *could* have killed you before he made his escape. Roger thinks he thought you were dead—or dying. We can't know for sure whether he did or not. But if he did, it would have to mean he had some other reason for wanting to escape. And if he didn't—wouldn't going outside and trying to

136

kill you by wrecking the machine or setting a fire be an insane thing to do—when he could so easily have done it inside the machine right after Roger let him out?"

"There's no question about that," Blakemore said. "But now he seems to be trying to destroy us all, if what you believe about him is true. Roger is sure he doesn't hate you and Gilda at all, quite the contrary. For all we know, he neither set the fire nor moved the machine. But if he did, something very strange must have happened to make him change his mind. I'm basing my decision on one of those two possibilities—nothing more. I'm going outside because we're in the deadliest kind of danger until I find out."

"No, Dan!" Helen Blakemore stumbled a little in her haste to grip him by the arm and swing him half-about, as if she felt if she did not look directly into his eyes her ability to sway him would dwindle and vanish. "If you go you'll never stop regretting it, because I won't be here when you get back. I mean that, Dan."

"I think you will, darling," Blakemore said. "Those flames outside aren't going to die out for an hour or so. I'm almost sure of that. And in an hour you can do a lot of sober thinking. It isn't my life alone that's threatened now, much as Malador seems to hate me. Philip said it was only natural for me to be more concerned about you than about anyone else.

"It's true, of course. I can't deny it. But there are five of us, not just you and the man you married. Each has a claim on the other. It will always be that way, I'm afraid, when people have shared great dangers, and have come to feel very close to one another.

"You'll have time to think it over, darling and change your mind about letting me go. I'm not worried at all about what your decision will be."

CHAPTER TWELVE

Blakemore descended first, with Tyson about eight feet above him, and this time the apprehension that had come upon him when he had first stared down into the sea of gigantic fronds and yard-wide blooms was of a different nature. He had no fear of sinking down into a bogginess that might be close to bottomless, or of stepping by accident into a yawning pit of emptiness, marked only by a blue-black, whorl-like swirling.

It was the fear of not being sure that a patch of ground that looked as if it were covered with a scattering of ashes might not turn into a bed of white-hot embers, concealed from view by a superficial layer of embers that had, in cooling, turned powdery white and dust-like.

Two-thirds of the vegetation directly below the machine had been so seared by the flames that only the blackened stalks of the great plants remained standing, like the trunks of titan oaks and cedars that had been lightning blasted. Most of them were as large as tree-trunks and a few were considerably larger. Between them were wide patches of bare earth not even covered with ashes, but brightly gleaming from the fire's scouring. All of the sogginess was gone, dried up by the intense heat that the conflagration had generated.

It was a fire-blackened wasteland for the most part, and yet Blackmore could not see beyond it even from the summit of the machine, for it was still fringed by a row of very tall plants that had escaped destruction. Their blossoms still swayed in the breeze that was blowing across the fire-ruined acreage in erratic gusts, exactly as it had done on Blakemore's first descent and nothing had marred a display of colors—vermillion and purple, orange and green—so bright that he had to shade his eyes when he stared at them.

Closer at hand the few blooms that still hung from the fire-ravaged stalks were withered or tarnished, and a few had collapsed into shriveled husks that looked not unlike gigantic peapods half-eaten away by swarms of locusts just as gigantic.

There were no insects flying through the air or alighting on the ravaged growths, but Blakemore did not think that in the least surprising, for insects were slow to return to regions made desolate, whether by fire, flood or earthquake.

He paused suddenly—he was half way to the ground now—looked up and gestured to Tyson. "We don't have to worry about snakes, I guess—but it's just as well to be careful. We don't know what might come crawling up out of a burrow that goes deep into the soil."

"Makes sense," Roger said. "I'll keep a sharp lookout."

In a moment they had both reached the ground and were staring around them. Roger transferred the heavy weapon that Malador had made the mistake of not taking with him—or had it been a mistake?—from his left to his right hand and gestured toward the tall growths that were blocking the view.

"We might as well keep walking straight ahead," he said. "The important thing right now is to get a wider view of our surroundings. There could be open countryside beyond this out-sized flower garden or just another garden. What do you think?"

"I'd prefer not to think," Blakemore said. "Just to walk, as you suggest."

It took them perhaps forty seconds to cross the ash-covered expanse of ground between the machine and the tall growths that hemmed it in in a half-arc that was not quite a semi-circle. They were careful not to step on the ashes, but to keep to the smooth patches that the flames had burnished. Once or twice they had to stop, and hopscotch from patch to patch.

They they were moving between the tall, unseared growths, and were so utterly dwarfed by them that they had the illusion, for a few more seconds, that they were advancing through the aisles of a tropical rain forest.

But when they finally emerged from between the outermost row of towering stalks—some were bright green and seemed bursting with sap and others were curiously mottled—not only did the rain forest illusion vanish, but the vista that stretched out before them was so unlike the region of gigantic blooms and fronds surrounding the ship that it was hard for Blakemore to believe that they could have existed side by side, in such close proximity that they could be thought of as brushing elbows.

It was a vista desolate beyond belief, stretching out for miles to a distant mountain that was aureoled in a thin grayish haze which hid its summit from view and obscured as well something gigantic and sharp-angled that bisected it from base to summit.

The vista did two things to Blakemore. It stirred memories deep in his mind that totally bewildered him, for he was quite sure that he had never seen the vista before and yet he had instantly recognized it.

The monoliths— There were at least fifty of them scattered across the plain that stretched from the mountain to where he was standing and he had a distinct recollection of having stood before three or four of them and examined the inscriptions which covered them.

The other thing that the vista did to Blakemore was

strike him speechless, so that Tyson had to tug at his arm to jog him back to attentiveness.

"I said that the important thing was to get a wider view of our surroundings," Tyson said. "But I didn't think it would be quite as wide as that. It's like walking out of a glass-walled hothouse with plants all around you and damp earth odors in your nostrils and finding yourself in the middle of the Sahara—or the Gobi. If it jolts you as much as it does me, it might be better if we just accepted the fact that talking about it would serve no useful purpose.

"I mean—how can we hope to find Malador out there —if he *is* out there. It's too vast an expanse. With so many places he could—"

If Tyson had planned ahead and decided at what precise moment it might be best to carry out his suggestion and fall completely silent it was hardly likely that he would have done so in the middle of a sentence. Yet fall silent he did. Or it might be more truly said that silence was forced upon him by the blinding flash of light that came into view on the plain about a hundred feet from where they were standing. It was followed by a deafening blast of sound.

The ground shook and Blakemore was hurled to his knees. Tyson swayed, but managed to stay on his feet by bending a little backwards and using Malador's heavy weapon as an equilibrium-maintaining aid.

Something that looked like a fireball arose from the region of the blast and went streaking overhead, zigzagging for a moment and then hanging suspended almost motionless high in the sky. For five or six seconds it remained motionless. Then it sped on again until it was hovering directly above the vegetation from which Blakemore and Tyson had emerged.

Then it was gone, vanishing as abruptly as a meteor burnt to a cinder in earth's upper atmosphere but leaving in its wake a trail of bright radiance that took longer to disappear.

Another blinding flash arose from the desolate plain and another fireball streaked across the sky, hovering precisely as the first one had done above the fire-ravaged vegetation when it had completed its zigzagging course, but vanishing just a little more slowly, as if a giant hand had closed over it, and some of the radiance had gone right on spilling out between the contracting fingers of the hand.

As Blakemore got unsteadily to his feet he was struck by the strange thought—strange at such a moment—that he had never before seen on a human face an expression quite like the one that had turned Tyson's features into a grotesque, almost aboriginal-like mask.

Not only was his face livid and the lines about his mouth abnormal in all respects. His lips were so tightly contracted that they must have been giving him pain and his eyes had a glassy, protruding look.

Just the fact that he had remained standing seemed to mean nothing at all to him, for he gripped Blakemore's arm the instant the latter regained his feet, as if he, and not Blakemore, were most in need of support.

"It's another attack on the machine," he muttered hoarsely. "I— I don't see anything out there. Do you? How do you explain it? That burst of flame seemed to come right up out of the ground."

"There's nothing moving out there, that's for sure," Blakemore heard himself replying. "We're too near to where that fireball came from to be mistaken about that.

"Fireball? Yes, that's what it looked like. Do you suppose it could be some kind of natural phenomenon? I was sure it had been fired from a weapon, but—I just don't know."

"I think it was fired deliberately," Blakemore said.

"Not at the machine, perhaps, but at us. That traveling ball of flame could well have missed its mark."

"What shall we do? Go back to the machine? I think we should."

Blakemore shook his head. "If the attack is being made on the machine—and we don't even know if it *is* an attack—we're not going to stop it by giving up what he came out here to do. We've got to get over to where that blast came from before we're blown apart."

"Are you crazy? When there's a blast like that you don't walk right toward where there could be another one at any moment. You get as far away from it as you can."

"There was just one blast, followed by two balls of flame," Blakemore said. "We'll wait a minute to see if another one comes. If it doesn't—I think we should take the risk. There are a few boulders out there—large ones. We can dodge and weave about until we get up close. There's no other way we can hope to put a stop to it."

"Well, all right," Tyson said, after a pause. "It isn't just taking a risk. It's making four-fifths sure there'll be a funeral cortege for both of us, but without a hearse. "I've often wondered what it would be like to be 'buried' that way, in shining fragments spread out across the sky."

"We may find out," Blakemore said. "But we've no choice. If we go back to the machine the attack will go on, and— Look, I said it may not be an attack. You think Malador is behind it. I've never been sure. We've got to settle it, once and for all. If it's a natural phenomenon it's not too likely to be repeated. How often do freakish lightning bolts, the kind that can fork down and kill you without harming a tree or a house, occur more than once in the same place? If it's a natural phenomenon we'll have nothing to worry about. But we've got to determine whether it is or not or everything will stay the way it was. It's not a good way to have everything stay."

They waited at least three full minutes before they left the shadows cast by the tall stalks at their backs and started out across the plain. They moved toward the nearest of the scattered boulders, almost but not quite running, for the ground was rugged underfoot and crouched down behind it for an instant before continuing on. It was perhaps a useless precaution, but it had occurred to Blakemore, as he had pointed out to Tyson, that a very large boulder might afford some protection if another blast came.

Whether it would have concealed them as well from watching eyes was a moot question, for their swift advance could hardly have remained unnoticed otherwise, unless the eyes had been trained in some other direction nine-tenths of the time.

There were five more boulders to pass, behind each of which they crouched briefly, exchanging glances that were meant to be self-congratulatory but could hardly have looked that way, before they came in sight of something that made them duck down behind the fifth boulder with their eyes widened in disbelief.

Projecting straight up out of the ground—or almost straight, since it was at a slight tangent—was a long, shining tube.

It seemed like no more than a tube at first, burnished a coppery bronze. Then they saw that it was smoke-blackened over a third of its length and bore a distinct resemblance to a weapon of large-scale warfare that had been used in the twentieth century over a span of more than twenty-five years. A *bazooka*. But no—it wasn't like that either. There was something about it that gave it more the look of a weapon that hadn't been invented yet —if by "yet" you meant as late as the early years of the twenty-first century.

There were some incredible outside gadgetry attached

144

to it near its base, so complex-looking that it made Blakemore's vision reel and seemed actually to hurt his eyes, precisely as the weapon which Tyson was now carrying seemed always to do whenever he stared at it for more than a few seconds. Except that the complexity was a great deal more pronounced than it was in the weapon they had taken away from Malador, and there was a glitter too, which made it even more difficult for him to keep staring at it.

"Well, that's it," Blakemore said, but with no note of triumph in his voice. "Apparently you and Philip were mistaken and I was right. Malador couldn't have hurled that fireball toward us—or the machine—just by monkeying around with the hidden powers of his mind. It came from that weapon, and he not only couldn't have known he'd find a weapon like that—if he *has* found it—but—well, can you picture him as discovering how to operate it fast enough to launch an attack on the machine in less than a half hour after he made his escape? I certainly can't."

"But if Malador didn't launch the attack, who did?" Tyson asked, and there was a shakiness in his voice that was so uncharacteristic of him that Blakemore preferred not to meet his gaze. No man likes it to be known that so great a shattering can take place in his mind that, if only for the barest instant, all of his courage recedes, like channels of water running with quicksilver speed down a slanting beach at ebbtide.

"That's what we're going to find out," Blakemore said. "There's nothing to be gained by putting it off."

"But it was just fired! There's no one in sight, but someone must have operated it."

"Malador could have fired it this time," Blakemore said. "He could have mastered its complexity by now. I don't think so, but it's remotely possible."

"Where is he then?"

"Underground—whether it's Malador or someone else.

Can't you see—the emplacement is just a shallow trench. A weapon that massive would have to have just as massive an operational base. The gadgetry at the base of the tube itself provides no solid support."

It took them only a moment to emerge from behind the boulder and advance to within a few feet of where the weapon towered.

They halted for an instant, but only long enough to confirm what Blakemore had been almost sure of. There was a cavernous opening in the earth immediately surrounding the tube, visible from where they were standing.

It completely encircled the tube, which jutted up at its precise center.

"What do we do now?" Tyson asked. "Go to the edge and look down? We'd better do that before we start down. There has to be someone at the bottom and he's not going to rush up and embrace us."

"We'll see," Blakemore said. "Keep a tight grip on that weapon. We may need it at any moment."

They moved forward again, and came to another halt at the edge of the cavernous opening. They could see nothing when they looked down—just a swirling darkness.

They were steps leading downward. That much they could tell despite the darkness, for the three uppermost ones stood out distinctly. The one at the top was even gilded by the sunlight.

They did not appear to be stone steps, and had a metallic luster.

"I'll go first," Blakemore said. "Stay about four feet behind me and make sure that you can bring that weapon to bear on anyone who leaps out at me. I hope that what Gilda said isn't true. That you *do* know how to operate it."

"I never told her that," Tyson said. "I swear it."

"But are you *sure* you can operate it?"

146

"No," Tyson said, with startling candor. "But I'm almost sure."

"You might have tried—just to make absolutely sure," Blakemore said. "Oh, well—"

"I was afraid to," Tyson said. "You told me he blasted with it three times, perhaps more. We don't know how many charges he may have used up before he brought your jet down. I might have wasted more than one in testing it out. No—it would have been foolish. There may not be any charges left as it is."

"That's a comforting thought," Blakemore said. "All right. We might as well start down."

They descended slowly and cautiously, testing the firmness and width of each step with their feet before leaving the one above. There were no handrails.

The emplacement seemed to go deep into the earth, and for close to half a minute they descended in absolute darkness. Then a faint glimmer of light became visible far below and grew swiftly brighter.

That would have been more reassuring than otherwise if something had not happened a few seconds after it became brighter that made Blakemore halt abruptly and stare with alarm at the shining tube.

The tube was moving very slowly back and forth, as if whoever might be operating the massive weapon was uncertain as to whether or not it should be fired again. It was almost as if there was a childish irresponsibility at work at the base of the weapon, a failure to understand that a weapon so formidable should not be operated in so erratic a way.

Just the fact that Blakemore was no longer outside on the plain, standing in the target area, did not mean that he had nothing to fear if the weapon went off again. The steps were so near to it that the heat of the firing alone might come close to incinerating him, if the concussion did not hurl him from the stairs.

Tyson had become aware of the danger too, and his

voice was sharp with alarm, though he managed to keep it low-pitched enough to avoid giving their presence away before they reached the lower-most step and could no longer hope to keep it concealed.

"If that weapon goes off now we could be killed," he said. "We're within three or four feet of it. The recoil alone—"

"I know," Blakemore said, cutting him short. "It means we've got to get down the rest of these steps fast. Proves one thing, though. That fireball was aimed at the machine, not at us."

They got down the rest of the steps fast and were moving out from the lowermost one when the great weapon went off with a thunderous roar.

They were hurled to the ground and before they could get to their feet again someone darted past them and started ascending the stairs as swiftly as they had descended.

The light was very bright and they caught no more than a fleeting glimpse of him amidst a dazzlement that half-blinded them. But that brief glimpse caused Blakemore to cry out in furious disbelief and Tyson to cry out also.

The swiftly vanishing figure was that of a naked child —a boy of not more than eleven or twelve at the most, his hair long and matted, and straggling down over his ears, his skin glinting berry-brown in the glare of what looked like a dozen crude oil lamps sending out smoky fumes. He was carrying a short, stone hatchet, which he did not relinquish as he fled.

"A barbarian child!" Tyson said, looking so stunned it surprised Blakemore he could speak at all. "A Stone Age child. How could he possibly have known how to operate—"

"A boy half his age—a child of four even—could fire almost any weapon with an uncomplicated trigger mechanism," Blakemore said. "The complexity of that one was apparently in the gadgetry on the tube and the precise technological function it was built to perform—perhaps a half million years ago.

"He was only a child," he went on thoughtfully. "But an *adult* on the rude barbarian level might well be able not only to fire it, but to turn it on a hated enemy, without knowing a thing about its technological complexity. And the machine, arriving as it did out of the blue, might have seemed to the barbarian inhabitants of this age the equivalent of a fiery dragon breathing out smoke and flames. So they tried to destroy it with fire from this weapon—not knowing, of course, that it was the kind of fire that could pass right through an opaque metal barrier as only infra-red and other kinds of invisible heat rays are supposed to be capable of doing, and still look like visible light."

"The boy we just saw wasn't a Stone Age youngster, I'm afraid. He's just a boy of the far future, when mankind's triumphs will have dwindled and vanished—as we now know, of course, they've done. We could hardly fail to know, since we're standing right in the midst of the tragic remnants. I would say that the remnants have a very frayed edge."

"And I thought it was Malador. I thought we'd find him here—not that boy."

"Malador is here," Blakemore said, gripping Tyson's arm, and pointing, his fingers tightening on the younger man's wrist like steel bands. "He couldn't have fired the weapon, however. Not with that spear in him."

Malador was lying on his back, half in shadows, with the crude oil lamps casting a flickering radiance over his head and shoulders. He was spread-eagled on a floor of smooth, but verdigris-encrusted metal, his eyes sightlessly staring and his arms stretched so wide they seemed to be wrenching to get out of their sockets, even in death.

A long gleaming spear, with a cluster of feathers attached to its hilt, protruded from almost the exact middle of his chest.

"God!" Tyson said, his voice choked. "You saw him and didn't tell me. You went right on talking—"

"I had a reason," Blakemore said. "There's nothing we can do for him now, and I don't want what happened to him to happen to us. I don't think they liked the interest he took in *their* weapon and that's why they killed him. It means we've got to get out of here fast. I had to make you see how important getting out fast is—just what it means to them to own a weapon like that."

"I think I get it," Tyson said. "You enraged Malador by growing a field of wheat and he enraged them just as much by violating a sacred tabu."

"Exactly," Blakemore said. "Now suppose we see how fast we can climb back out and get back to the machine. Any minute now they may discover that we've enraged them too. Just one look at that kid gives me a pretty good idea what the adults must be like. A stone hatchet at twelve might not be so bad in itself, compared to some of war-game toys kids that age played with in the past. But there was blood on it. Or didn't you notice?"

"No, I didn't notice," Tyson said. "Freshly shed?"

"I think so. It could be animal blood, of course. A fine, brave little hunter. But if there are warring tribes in this age—"

"Come on," Tyson said. "Let's go."

CHAPTER THIRTEEN

It happened more swiftly—and unexpectedly—than Blakemore and Tyson had feared that it might, and they had feared that it might not be long in coming.

The skin-clad barbarians—or were they savages?—emerged from behind a dozen boulders the instant Tyson's head came into view and while Blakemore was still four steps lower down.

They came swarming over a slight rise in the landscape as well, some swinging stone axes and others armed with spears. They were not in the least Neanderthal-like in aspect, for the one thing that man had apparently not done in regressing culturally was circle back on the course of human evolution. They were sturdily built and tall in stature, clad for the most part in the skins of animals, although a few were totally naked.

They were not tribally well-organized and had seemingly no great skill in warfare, for they converged on the massive weapon singly and in pairs, waving their arms as they ran and occasionally taking long leaps that somehow failed to enable them to cover the intervening distance much faster.

A few bore themselves with more dignity and had more the look of seasoned warriors.

What saved Blakemore and Tyson from an immediate hand-to-hand encounter at the base of the weapon and enabled them to postpone it was the fact that the running tribesmen nearest to the weapon did not move *quite* fast enough.

It was a simple enough circumstance, but one which, across the ages, has determined the destiny of millions of individuals and not a few nations, and not always in the realm of warfare.

In a moment they were both several yards from the weapon and running across the plain just as fast, Blakemore found himself hoping, as the nearest of the pursuing tribesmen, who were comparatively few in number.

But their numbers swelled rapidly and when Blakemore glanced back for the second time—his first glance had been reassuring—he realized that he could not hope to outdistance them until he reached the machine. There were too many very rapid runners.

"You've got to use Malador's weapon," he said, pausing for the barest instant to bring Tyson to a halt. "Turn around, take careful aim and see what you can accomplish. You don't have to blast them down. It's crazy, I know—I ought to have my head examined. But it's the way I feel about it."

"What do you suggest I do?" Tyson demanded. "It *is* crazy, when it's our lives or theirs."

"Blast the earth directly in front of them," Blakemore told him. "Rip a big trench in it, if you can. It's not their fault they've regressed to barbarism."

"Oh, all right. But it's madness."

Tyson was raising the weapon, his hands busy on the trigger mechanism which no child could possibly have operated when two hurled spears went spinning over their heads, making Blakemore almost regret what he'd told the other not to do.

"In another moment we'll have spears sticking out all over us," Tyson muttered. "You'll be as sorry as hell and you won't get any sympathy from me. I'll be too dead to extend it."

"Shut up and take careful aim. Hurry. If you can't work it—I'll try. It's got to be done fast."

Tyson had the weapon at shoulder level now. But Blakemore had no idea what was going to happen. Probably Tyson would blast to kill and apologize afterwards, but he'd done all he could to prevent it. His conscience was clear and he could sleep nights, but he was probably a fool in the bargain.

The weapon seemed to come to life in Tyson's hands an instant before a long tongue of flame darted from it, followed by a deafening roar.

Though Blakemore was standing within four feet of him only his ears were deafened. There were no displaced currents of air lashing against him, nothing to indicate that a hand weapon more powerful than the gunmakers of the twenty-first century would have been able to construct in a lifetime of trying had gone off that close to him. Except that, when he looked down, he saw that Tyson had been hurled to the ground and was just struggling to a sitting position, the weapon still in his clasp.

Directly in front of him a thick curtain of smoke obscured what had happened. But it thinned out very quickly and he saw that Tyson had accomplished exactly what he had urged him to at least attempt. The ground immediately in front of the pursuing tribesmen had been ripped apart in eight or ten places and from the dust-filled craters which had been blasted out of the soil thin columns of smoke were still arising.

The tribesmen had scattered. Some had turned and fled, shrieking in terror. Others were climbing out of the craters, their faces smoke-blackened and looking as if they would have no heart for continuing on in pursuit of men they had made the mistake of thinking less than god-like.

But there was one who seemed undaunted, both by

the yawning craters and the demoralization which had followed in the wake of the blast.

He leapt straight across the narrowest of the craters and came rushing straight toward Blakemore with his spear extended.

Blakemore waited until he was within four feet of him, then sidestepped the spear, brought his right hand up in a chopping motion no different from the one he had used to keep Tyson from committing an act of suicidal folly and finished with a blow that would have disqualified him if he had been a professional boxer. But deep in every man, Blakemore knew, there was a buried savage and if ever there was a right time to resurrect him it was now.

The tribesman crumpled as if a wedge of steel had slammed into him. Blakemore bent and picked up the spear, which had gone spinning.

He hoped he wouldn't need it, for Tyson was on his feet now, and they were both in good mettle to make a final run for it.

He hoped he wouldn't need it—and he didn't. What could not have been more than three minutes later they were ascending into the machine, with no one at all in pursuit of them.

Before they passed inside Tyson paused just long enough on the topmost rung to ask: "Why do you suppose Malador wanted to bring down the thunder? He must have known what he'd be walking into. Whatever you may think about the extent of his paranormal gifts you'll have to admit that they were unusual. He must have known exactly what those barbarians would be capable of."

"He may have felt he was no longer among friends, exactly," Blakemore said. "In a way, I feel sorry for him. He thought I was dead or dying and hating me was no longer something that could make him forget almost everything else. He just didn't want to remain in captivity. He hoped to find a new world outside that he could reshape, a world that would enable him to live a richer, fuller and more abundant life than he had known in the twenty-second century. Wretchedness and starvation can make a man desperate, willing to take any risk to achieve something better."

CHAPTER FOURTEEN

Blakemore doubted if he would have been capable of performing a miracle and keeping it as closely guarded a secret as Faran had done.

He doubted also that he could have revealed the wonder of it in quite so dramatic a way.

Faran didn't just walk into the viewing window compartment and say: "I knew I could do it. All I needed was a little more time. I won't pretend I wasn't afraid we might be stranded here forever until I got down to really studying the dials. But then I knew, it came to me."

He didn't say that at all. All he said was: "In just about four more minutes you'll be taking your last look at our flower garden—or what's left of it. When we come back —and I think we will—there isn't one chance in a thousand we'll come out tangential to the warp field at exactly this spot."

No one spoke, no one said a word, because there are times when no one can, when speech becomes impossible. Blakemore could understand that and had no wish to change it. He might have said a few words, he felt, by making a supreme effort, but he preferred not to.

They saw it perhaps twenty seconds—not longer—— after the machine had been set in motion.

They were all standing directly in front of the viewing

window when the mountain came clearly into view, and they saw the Great Stone Face.

It could have been carved out of basalt or quartz crystal or some other, unknown mineral. What it had been carved out of didn't seem to matter.

Helen Blakemore cried out and then remained motionless, standing as still as the carved figure, which must have been at least a thousand feet in height, because it was the same height as the mountain.

Blakemore blinked, then swayed a little.

Tyson said: "After a half million years—"

It was Gilda who broke the spell. "You look a little pale, Dan. But it's a wonderful likeness all the same. Isn't it, Dad?"

"Yes, it is," Faran said. "And it makes what I'm going to say—well, this is the right time to say it, I think.

"We saw the shining cities—we saw what Dan's wheat made possible. But that, too, had to come to an end because the human clock ran down. Man's energies simply gave out. Almost everyone knew it would be that way—the wisest philosophers simply saw it more clearly than most.

In this age man is on his way to extinction. It is really all over, or soon will be. But time travel and what Dan has done—can change all that.

Don't you see? There can be another beginning, a new blueprint for the human race. We can build more machines like this and save the bravest and the best—from a hundred different ages—and set the clock to ticking again, a half million years in the future.

"We can and we will," Dan said. "But there's only one thing—that face out there should be yours, not mine."

"I like Dad's face just the way it is," Gilda said. "It has a comfortable, fatherly look. But on you—both faces look good."

FANTASY-ADVENTURE'S
GREATEST HERO

Readers and critics have long considered the tales of Conan to be among the greatest fantasy-adventure epics of all time, comparable to E. R. Eddison, J. R. R. Tolkien and Edgar Rice Burroughs. Lancer is proud to present the complete Conan series in uniform editions.

CONAN THE WARRIOR	73-549	60¢
CONAN THE CONQUEROR	73-572	60¢
CONAN THE AVENGER	73-780	60¢
CONAN OF THE ISLES	73-800	60¢
CONAN THE WANDERER	74-976	95¢
CONAN OF CIMMERIA	75-072	95¢
CONAN THE ADVENTURER	75-102	95¢
CONAN THE USURPER	75-103	95¢
CONAN	75-104	95¢
CONAN THE FREEBOOTER	75-119	95¢

Look for the special display of these titles at your local newsstand or bookstore. If not available there, send the price of each book you desire, plus 10¢ per book to cover mailing costs, to LANCER BOOKS, INC., 1560 Broadway, New York, N.Y. 10036. On orders of four or more books, Lancer will pay the postage.

The Great
Science Fiction
Comes from Lancer!

Have you missed any of these recent bestsellers?

(Cont. on next page)

More Great
Science Fiction
from Lancer!